ARTIST
AT WAR

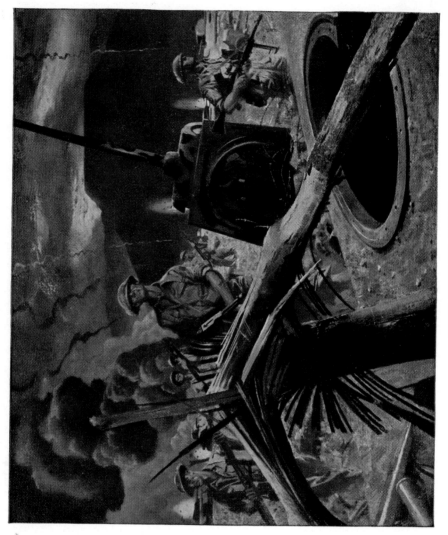

THE HITLER LINE

ARTIST AT WAR

CHARLES FRASER COMFORT
R.C.A., O.S.A.

THE RYERSON PRESS - TORONTO

Published October, 1956

ACKNOWLEDGMENT

Frontispiece, Courtesy Canadian War
Collection, The National Gallery. All
other illustrations courtesy of the Direc-
torate of Public Relations, Canadian
Army, Ottawa.

PRINTED AND BOUND IN CANADA
BY THE RYERSON PRESS, TORONTO

To
Louise, Ruth and Anne

Foreword

A momentous and troubled decade has passed since the cease fire. It would seem reasonable to presume that today it becomes necessary to offer an apology for any book that has as its background the Second World War. This would seem increasingly so as that conflict recedes into deepening perspectives. Yet for many, as for me, that experience, in all its dramatic intensity, seems removed from the normal context of time and, with the passage of years, becomes isolated in a dimension of its own.

This is an account of my personal experiences during an episode of that war. I have undertaken to write these rambling, discontinuous, impressions because I was profoundly stirred by all that I saw and felt during that experience. I must confess that I have been driven to the task by a sort of nostalgic compulsion that I have found difficult to deny and have possibly been ill-advised to follow.

This is not a history of the campaign, I leave that problem to my colleagues, the historians. My hope has been to present an objective narrative, based on individual perception, and upon sources of information available at the time and then considered to be fact. What I saw or was eye-witness to is reliably accounted for here. But there was much that I heard, or was told at the time, rumours and colourful fantasies, which, in the light of later evidence, have been shown to depart somewhat from what did occur. Yet I have not hesitated to use such information because it has been my intention, if possible, to recapture the quality of feeling experienced at the time. Surely much would be missed, if such material were omitted from a personal account.

The part I played was a minor and inconspicuous one. I was not a combat soldier, although I had been trained as such, but a war artist, assigned the task of producing some visual record of the part played by officers and men of the 1st Canadian Infantry Division during the Italian campaign of 1943-44, an appointment which offered me opportunities for observation, not only of many of the actions, but of the quality of appearances in Italy at the time.

My relationship to all ranks of the Division was of the friendliest character, in fact I was one of them. I am proud to have served with so gallant and unforgettable a company, to have been eye-witness to their fine achievement, their suffering, and their brave sacrifice in the cause of liberty. With respect and gratitude, I pay my small tribute to those who did not return, as well as to those who survived.

CHARLES COMFORT.

The Studio Building,
Toronto, 1956.

Introduction

By Eric Harrison

My friendship with Charles Comfort was kindled at our first encounter. It was a festive occasion with everybody dressed up for the opening of Strachan Hall, that felicitous essay in the gothic at Trinity College, Toronto. The shift of scene, in little more than a year, from Trinity to the tents at Marino di San Vito, was a shocking one, an abrupt change of mood from happiness to horror. The academic civilities belonged to another existence. By the quaking shore of the Adriatic men and the elements, each hating the other, had conspired to create an infernal fifth dimension, plumbing not life but death. It was in circumstances of overwhelming and malignant violence, of fear, cold, and spiritual unease that I caught up with Charles. It was before Ortona on Christmas Day, 1943. Posterity will read his description of that Canadian battle against the German paratroopers with awe. No one has written of it more vividly.

Yet Comfort's mission with the 1st Canadian Infantry Division in Italy was not as a writer but as a soldiering artist. With the rank of a Captain in the Historical Section of the General Staff, he had been attached to the divisional head-quarters for the purpose of making a painter's record in the theatre of war. He had a forerunner in that unusual adventure, his friend, Will Ogilvie, who went in with the troops for the Sicilian landings. Will's manly capability in the performance of a duty, so oddly detached from the fighting, yet in such hazardous communion with it, set a standard for us all. He was able to pass on his experience of pioneering in the work; and Comfort's devotion to the task under harsh conditions had its precedent in Ogilvie's example. Undaunted by Italy, they were both to apply their skills and their courage with the Army in north-west Europe when the time came.

It has always been part of my good fortune in life to be a friend of artists. I married one. It is a unique indebtedness. For as my masters at school taught me to read, my artist friends have taught me to see. They have not given me the analytical and commanding visions of a painter, confident in perception and technique. But at least they have cured me from being purblind to some of the facts before me, the plasticity of rock or tree, the complex revelation of a face, the colour of a mood, the absoluteness of a wooden chair.

I was to continue this training in awareness during my service in Italy. Comfort became my principal teacher, but attached with him to our 1st Division for a time was Lawren Harris, gifted son of a famous father, whose diction in that phase of his career as a painter in oils was Florentine— fastidious, immaculate, sardonic, ruthless, macabre. There were to be two other artists working under my general direction in Italy, Campbell Tinning, who brought a wayward lyric touch after Harris' black realism with the 5th Canadian Armoured Division, and Tom MacDonald, whose painting, in the wake of Comfort with the infantry, was as forthright as his name and as sterling as the man himself. I had cause to be grateful to them all, not only for showing me their several ways of looking at war in a storied land, but for their cheerful acceptance of my administrative responsibility for them amidst the strains and deprivations of the field.

My official concern with the War Artists was as a sort of manager and impresario. I was sent to the Mediterranean as Historical Officer with Headquarters 1st Canadian Corps under Lt.-General Crerar, and as O.C. 1st Canadian Field Historical Section, an exiguous command of specialists, with a war establishment at that stage hardly existing even on paper, and for which bodies and equipment had to be "scrounged" in a theatre denuded of everything moveable by our predecessors, whether enemies or allies. It speaks well for my upbringing that not until I became a captain in the army did I learn to steal.

The detail of our requirements was being worked out in London by Captain Sesia, who had accompanied Ogilvie through the campaign in Sicily and thus found out what was required to set us up as a mobile unit in the field. As an Historical Officer, Gus Sesia enjoyed the reputation of having made a faithful and even lurid transcription of everything he saw and heard. When I arrived, he had been relieved at divisional headquarters by Captain Sam Hughes, wearer of an historic name, and one of the liveliest minds it has ever been my pleasure to know. As was to be expected, he had strong political views, and I heard with sympathy that it was his intention after the war to reform the Conservative Party. I first discovered Sam in the appalling situation in front of Ortona, reading Gibbon by the light of a hurricane lantern.

The times were hard for artists and historians alike, but the authorities were with us, and eventually we got our tents and jeeps and portable typewriters, and "G Hist." came to look like the going concern it had proved itself to be. General Crerar and his successor as Corps Commander, Lt.-General Burns, were most helpful, both of them having urged when the war broke out that proper attention be given to the maintenance of the historical record. It was as a result of such representations that Lt.-Colonel Stacey had come to preside over the Historical Section of the General Staff at Canadian Military Headquarters in London, a scholar of outstanding capacity, and the *deus ex machina* whom I invoked when in despair. No commander in the field was more inisistent on the appointment of an Historical Officer to his formation than Major-General Simonds when getting the 5th Armoured Division ready to move into the line. No formation put in stronger requests for the attachment of Historical Officer and

War Artist than the 1st Canadian Armoured Brigade which, under Brigadier Murphy, fought so well in support of the British infantry, sometimes hundreds of miles away. The best officers and the most efficient units were the keenest to submit the evidence of their success or failure to the judgment of time. Their confidence was the measure of their morale. Few histories have had their materials garnered so close on the ripening of action, perishables scorchingly snatched from the furnace of war.

None was more eager to limn the very flame of it than Charles Comfort. On occasion he was more exposed than the fighting-men themselves. But for weeks together he existed in places that were under the guns, sharing precarious space between canvas and mud with Hughes and Harris, and quick resort by day or dark to the slit-trench, repellent with water. He could be too shaken while sketching to give the whole of himself to the act of contemplation and reduction. I found myself marvelling at his ability to stand still at his portable easel in weather too raw for me to do anything but move about in an effort to stir the circulation. Yet his sketches always showed what I had failed to see. They were performed with that capacity to select and interpret, comment and trans-literate, which is the refined product of his schooling and experience; and though the mind driving the hand might be distraught, the brushes' statement expounded what perception knew to be there, the craftsman obeying the artist with the instinct of a trained soldier to do what must be done in the crisis of action, swiftly, precisely, triumphantly. The form, texture, colour and function of what Comfort saw flowed in with his washes: they conveyed also what men might feel who were observers with him.

This habit of order is characteristic of his method. It illumines his book. Major Comfort, as he deservedly became, knew that he was being an eye-witness to history, and with sight like crystal, he was also an avid recorder. No detail escaped his note-taking, and I often deplored my own tendency to rely on a blurring memory in half-tone as contrasted with the faithful tablets of my polychromatic colleague. The outcome in the following pages is a brilliantly articulated documentary, re-creating the experience of the artist as he campaigns through that disturbed but still eternal storehouse of the European genius. All who were there will recall the like of these sights and sounds. There can be few passages in prose where the concatenated argument of the guns has been as ingeniously conveyed to eardrums that have forgotten the noise, the identities and the terror of it. The livid horror of "Morning Glory," the "tumultuous, triumphant inventiveness" of the Basilica of St. Peter, thus held in the erudite contemplation of the artist at the High Mass celebrated for the Royal 22nd Regiment; Adriatic sleet and Tyrrhenian sunshine, the white crosses for the Edmontons and the Seaforths, the sombre rubble of Pontecorvo, the dead in the Liri valley; indescribable Cassino; the grey olives and the incredible, fungoid hill-towns of the mediæval Apennines—the beauty, the misery, the night-mare by daylight that were the campaign in Italy: this is the stuff of a modern van Orley's tapestry of a new Pavia. Think of having such a book for the Seven Years' War or the War of 1812! And what material for a chapter in the history of Canadian painting!

For me to think that Comfort will be read by the curious a hundred years hence is only to regret that future generations will see me as a "sculptural freak", cavorting in the Tiber. But for posterity's sake I must forgive this ambidextrous man, brush in one hand, pen in the other, and commend the writing of a distinguished painter as adding a rarity to our literature.

Contents

CHAPTER   PAGE

Foreword vii

Introduction by W. E. C. Harrison, O.B.E., M.A.,
    Head of Department of History, Queen's University   ix

PART I

THE APPROACH MARCH 1
    S.S. Volendam 1
    In the Cork Forest 9
    Landing Craft Infantry 15
    North through Puglia 19

PART II

THE CAMPAIGN 27
    Campobasso 27
    Naples, November 40
    Campobasso II 44

PART III

ORTONA 60
    Hiatus 116
    The Liri Valley 136
    Rome, June 152
    Rome, July 161
    Florence, August 169
    Withdrawal 173

List of Illustrations

FACING
PAGE

The Hitler Line . . . . *Frontispiece*

Canadian Troops aboard Transport *Volendam*.
S.S. *California* on left 14

Philippeville, North Africa. Cape de Fer
and Stora Bay in background . . . 15

American L.C.I. Transporting Canadian Troops
from Philippeville, Algeria, to Taranto, Italy.
Mount Etna, Sicily, in background . . . 46

"Stand Easy" Following Crash Action . . . 47

Canadian Field Guns near Ortona . . . 78

Piazza Plebiscito, Ortona 79

Piazza San Francesco di Assisi. Wrecked Church
of Santa Maria Della Grazie, Ortona . . 110

Battle Scene—(Fantasy)—Villa Grande Road . . 111

Rocca San Giovanni, looking north . . . 142

Aquino, Italy 143

Route 6 at Cassino 174

Destroyed Panzertrum on the Adolf Hitler Line . 175

PART

I

THE APPROACH MARCH

S.S. Volendam:

Gulls mew in the shrill air, soar, dive, glide and mew—mew—mew. We are standing out into the Irish Sea. Occasional beams of peaked sunshine sweep the chill waters, heightening the drama of the occasion. The ack-ack towers gawk blindly at us, waist deep, like diplodoci feeding at the river's mouth. The tilted, half-submerged wrecks, like partially devoured carcasses, lie silent and abandoned.

Our ships, in two columns, were beating across a lively chop to a rendezvous with the Gourock convoy somewhere off the north coast of Ireland. Wind-hollows formed in the cheeks, trouser legs snapped like signal flags at the masthead. An escort vessel ploughed and rolled deeply to starboard, behind us Snowdon's high crest and the headlands of Anglesea receded into the advancing night. Adventure had begun, and with it that quality of lively excitation which surrounds the beginnings of every fresh wartime experience. The ship

1

vibrated with the combustion of high spirits, expressed in laughter, appetites, profane anecdote, and lusty song:

> Roll out the barrel,
> Let's have a barrel of fun.
> Roll out the barrel,
> We've got the Hun on the run . . .

The depressing inactivity of waiting has ended. We are under way, we are moving, moving toward who knows what? Uncomfortable, yes, no one would willingly choose to live cooped up for days like rush-hour travellers in a London tube, but the Prime Minister had recenty directed, because of the acute shortage of shipping, that every available space on troop-ships must be filled. There was no questioning the fact, in our case, that the Embarkation Officer had taken this injunction literally. But no one cared or complained; we were escaping the empty listlessness of just hovering in suspension in the fog-bound Mersey, as well as the trying uncertainties of Aldershot. Early tomorrow we should enter a new front-line situation, but we "couldn't care less!" From the troop decks a raucous chorus swelled in distorted echoes:

> Bless them all, bless them all,
> The long and the short and the tall . . .

The boat cleaves the sea with steady power, heaving imperceptibly. An occasional seventh wave crashes the bow, shoots high into the air and is carried across the streaming decks by the strong cross-wind. The port oerlikon gunners for'ard, and the moving groups of troops, are drenched by flying spray. As the afternoon declines, the solid western overcast creeps nearer, combining with the approaching dusk to hide us from the world.

*   *   *

Just a fortnight ago I had been ordered to report to No. 1, C.G.R.U., Aldershot. It seemed that an endless frustrating eternity of time had passed since then, yet it was only a fortnight. Parades, roll calls, twenty-four hour warnings, medicals, dental, pay, quartermaster, off-warning, serials cancelled, rumours and alarms, raised and shattered our hopes in endless sequence.

On my second morning at Aldershot, Sam Hughes appeared in Room 8. He was an amazingly spirited young man and I appreciated that fact from the moment I met him. He and I were to form a team in the field, a sub-unit of a future Field Historical Section. But in Aldershot we were orphans, "odds and sods." "Historical Officers?" Who had ever heard of such? Plainly the O.C. General Company was perplexed, and so were we. Destined for service with the Central Mediterranean Force, it was his duty to dispatch us to that theatre with as little delay as possible; we were determined, like everyone else, that there should be no delay at all. We acted with unconcern, but when forty-eight hours had passed without our being assigned serial numbers, Hughes went to work on our problem at the very highest level.

*   *   *

The blackout had gone on during the evening meal and the spirits of the human cargo had banked down a bit. The gusty darkness of the weather deck was relieved by the flashing lights at the entrance to Belfast Lough and the Mull of Galloway. It was just possible to make out the positions of the nearest vessels. The escort rolled deeply a thousand yards dead ahead of us, *Reine del Pacifico* was a barely perceptible silhouette to port.

The interior of the ship had all the appearances of an over-crowded ant-hill. Khaki-clad men surged in all directions, the congestion increased by the standing order which required them to carry a Board of Trade life jacket, complete with red shoulder light, emergency rations, and a filled water bottle, at all times. Although we had been aboard for days, instructions and orders still blared out over the public address system: "Will the commander of serial number four-oh-two oblique

stroke nine-eight report immediately to the Ship's Orderly
Room."

I had an insipid gingerbeer in the smoke-filled officers'
lounge. The ship was bone dry but I noticed above the bar a
fascinating price list, not yet one year old. Some of the items
seemed incredible: Champagne per bottle, eleven and six; half,
six shillings. Sherry, sevenpence per glass; bottle, five and six.
Whiskey, six shillings; glass, sixpence. Liqueur Brandy, ten-
pence per glass. And so on. Not only had these prices no
relationship to those currently asked in London, but their very
existence seemed as legendary as Jove's nectar. I finished my
gingerbeer and made my way toward A.10. From the troop
decks could be heard a subdued and nostalgic chorus:

> You are my sunshine,
> My only sunshine,
> You make me happy
> When skies are gray . . .

Hughes and I had no alternative when we reported to
Aldershot. "General Company" was a heterogeneous formation, consisting of officer types in flux, all sizes, all callings,
doctors, paymasters, dentists, provosts, clergymen, and now
historian and artist. Regimentally speaking, we made a sorry
showing. For a guardsman, like Hughes, it must have been
a humiliating experience.

On the ninth day we learned that at long last we had been
assigned serial numbers, that meant there was some hope of
our getting out of the place: Hughes' finagling was proving
successful.

On the morning of the eleventh day, while Hughes
and I were struggling into full marching order for the 0830
parade, Mr. Fairley appeared and informed us that we were
to skip the regular parade and appear an hour later. It was
true enough, Hughes had been made O.C. of his own private
serial and I was to go with him.

Maida Parade Square disclosed the nature of our command: one Officer and thirty-nine Other Ranks of the Canadian

Provost Corps! A smarter and more formidable group of men it would be difficult to imagine. They towered over us, bursting with physical well-being—their officer, a strapping young Mounted Policeman, Lieutenant G. R. Mudge. The General Company commander informed us that we moved off that evening, parading at 1700 hours, and that we were to be inspected by the Reinforcement Unit Commander immediately. Mudge turned over to Hughes and Hughes ordered Mudge and me to the right flank of the party and stood us all at ease.

Up to this point I had known Hughes only as a spirited companion, with a refreshing sense of humour and a staggering knowledge of history. He was of average size, with a spare athletic body, lean intelligent face, rather thick steel-rimmed glasses, thinning wispy brown hair, thin for one so young. But the army was in his blood: he knew all that should be known about it and a great deal more. At that moment the inspecting officer and his party appeared and Sam's voice thundered across the square: "Provost party . . . Ah-tenn-SHUN! Open-order MARCH!"

*   *   *

By morning we had made the turn into the Atlantic. A raw wind howled and sighed in the rigging as a few silent gulls glided in the vicinity of the galley disposal hatches. Behind us, and receding fast, were the last headlands of Donegal and Londonderry. Our escort was dotted about the horizon, hulls up one moment, down the next.

A most ludicrous thing had happened. The O.C. Troops, having noted that a party of Provost had come aboard, lost no time in calling their serial commander, Captain S. H. S. Hughes, C.A.C., to his orderly room and appointing him Provost Marshal of the ship; automatically Mr. Mudge and I became his assistants. Fortunately, Mr. Mudge was a Royal Canadian Mounted Policeman and, in addition to his vast

knowledge of the law and its administration, we had three
extraordinarily skilled Sergeants.

*   *   *

After sailing west for two days, we gradually edged round
to the south, in a wide arc. The Provost duties proved strange
but not too trying. Mudge was a well-trained, efficient officer,
unceasing in his vigil and concern for the welfare of the ship
and ever mindful of his own N.C.O's and men. Naturally, he
was curious, in a friendly sort of way, about Hughes and me,
but a discreet reticence prevented his satisfying his curiosity all
at once. He did, however, chip away at the mystery and must
eventually have pieced together considerable information. He
was fascinated to learn that I was an artist, a vocation
shrouded in mystery for him, which could only be equalled by
my ignorance of the inner workings of his calling.

*   *   *

Neither Hughes nor I knew what to expect when we
reached Division. We knew we were increment, but what the
physical setup would be remained obscure. Capt. A. T. Sesia
and Lieut W. A. Ogilvie had landed with the invading forces
in Sicily, as Historical Officer and War Artist respectively.
How they had managed to fullfil their function under conditions of actual warfare remained as yet unknown to us.

The third day out I decided to make inquiry about painting, which was after all my primary duty. The raw gusty
weather would not permit more than brief sketches at that
time, but it might be possible as we went further south. On
the Atlantic crossing I had been sternly refused permission to
either paint or sketch, in spite of all the directives I carried,
commanding me to do so. I now approached the O.C. Canadians, Major Stewart Jones, and asked that he present my
request to the O.C. Ship and the Ship's Master. He was very
pleasant about the matter, in fact, even while suppressing a
trace of embarrassment, quite intelligently interested. I may

do him an injustice, but I thought I knew what was passing through his mind, I had heard officers say it: "What the hell has come over the Army? They'll be sending us ballet dancers next!" I gave him my file of credentials and crossed my fingers.

To my pleasant surprise, the O.C. Ship, Colonel Ward-Walker, came to my table at dinner time, greeted me with a smile and said, "By all means do your painting, and do try to get a sketch of the old man," meaning the Captain.

*   *   *

Fourteen troops ships and eight destroyers ease along in a southerly direction, visibility unlimited. We must be nearing the defile of the Straits. Light nimbuses float through a sky brilliant with sunlight. Tropical kit is optional today, tomorrow it is obligatory. Those of us with deck watch duties are alert, we have reason to be watchful and concerned. The assault convoy, bound for Sicily, lost three vessels in this area. We scan the glaring sea silently.

*   *   *

We have been at sea six days. Land birds continue to appear. The "Hoopoe" is a surprise, big as a Jay, black and white barred wings, with a red crested head. A turtle dove too is an oddity. Shore birds, like curlews and sandpipers, fuss about but still there is no land in sight.

The strong easterly still freshens, seas of mounting power crash broadside against the ship, raising her over the crests in gargantuan heaves. She twists and rolls in the troughs, tossing geysers of salty spray as high as the bridge, the green wake of the *Cameronia* cutting across our zig-zag path.

*   *   *

It turned out a day of lively action. It was rumoured at lunch table that King Peter of Jugoslavia was travelling with us, aboard *Reine del Pacifico*. I dismissed the idea as characteristic of shipboard rumour. It was not until weeks later that I heard that the young Jugoslav monarch was in Cairo, and had actually travelled in convoy with us.

The Oerlikons and Bofors swing to cover the heavy bass-viol drone of aircraft. A single four-engined plane appears, circling the Commodore. There is an exchange of aldus light signals and he is gone again. Follows a succession of flag signals, given and acknowledged. We must be approaching the straits. . . .

The Orderly Corporal roused us for the passage of the straits at 0345 hours. The scene on the boat deck was unforgettable: The convoy was proceeding, line ahead, along a path of moonlight, the ships darkly silhouetted against the shimmering sea. A low brilliant moon hung upside down in the eastern heavens, the constellation of Orion to the right of it, the Pleiades in the zenith. The roller-coaster Moroccan hills formed the southern horizon, with strings of tiara-like lights marking Tangier. A lighted city! Strange and wonderful to see in that far-away moonlight. The Gibraltar side was obscurely dark, a few points of light and a flashing beacon marking the shore. As we progressed down the channel, the long ridge of the heights became visible, a coverlet of cloud hiding the crest. I watched the scene with consuming interest. We were in the Mediterranean.

*   ⁂   *

This is the vulnerable area. The sun has just risen, glowing like a Roman candle behind a broken cloud bank. We are closed up again, *Bergensfiord* ahead and to starboard, *Dunnottar Castle* to port. Astern, an unidentified aircraft carrier. Barrage balloons, like huge carp, float idly above each vessel, mare's tails sweep the sky. Gunners are alerted, destroyers much closer in. Away to the south, the rolling hills of Algeria rim the skyline, faintly blue. This is the vulnerable area,

Deciding that the weather would never be more ideal for my work, I have commenced a painting on the boat-deck starboard. Tropical kit is in wear, shorts, bush-shirts, half hose. A fierce sun blazes out of a cloudless sky. The lounges are empty and all ranks sun-bathe on the weather decks. A week has wrought this miracle.

The coastal hills waver under wreaths of nimbuses, hanging below their crests. They have some semblance to our Coast Range, except for their sparse forestry. Dolphins play about the bow-wave, leaping and diving with effortless ease. Algiers is left behind, creeping up the slopes of low hills, buildings of seeming sky-scraper proportions piled up and up like children's blocks. Four of our convoy turned and left us here.

The coast withdraws into the southern mists and we are at sea again, out of the sight of land. A hot, hot night, like a summer's evening in the garden at home, heavy with the rosy scent of full-blown peonies, and a robin's song in the maples. The for'ard hold deck is filled with hatless open-shirted men. In the dusk they achieve extraordinary choral harmony:

> The bells are ringing
> For me and my gal . . .

In the Cork Forest:

We have been at sea for nine days. Now, here is Africa, teeming with irrepressible life, yet empty as the moon. We are about a mile off shore, anchored in the wide crescent of Stora Bay. A newly-risen sun is blazing over madder-coloured hills. Philippeville terraces above an incandescent sea, gleaming whitely in the hot sunshine. The low coastal hills are sparsely wooded, with what appears to be a coarse shrubbery. All but *Bergensfjord* and *Volendam* have passed on to the east: we move slowly in toward the quay, pontoons are floated alongside and made fast.

The town is a curious confusion of debonair white French Colonial buildings, and shabby sort of Provincial Moslem. The minaret of a mosque rises in isolation from behind the hill. To the west is the fort, to the east a Zouave barracks, all quivering in the mounting heat. We are ordered to the troop decks. The Sergeants, Meldrum, Williams and Murray, like all good Sergeants, have the Provost Serial readied to debark. Zero is notified at 1110 hours.

*   *   *

Hughes and I stagger off ahead of our party in full kit, web binding and chafing, lurching down the ramp to the pontoons and along the quay to a convoy of "Limey" trucks, scarcely noticing the strain and the heat. The harbour is fascinating. Arab dhows, French gunboats, R.A.F. rescue craft, the strange language, decayed fruit smells, native stevedores in filthy red fezzes, baggy pantaloons and bare feet.

Standing in open trucks, we are off up the Rue Clemenceau, an impressive boulevard in the nineteenth century style. The transverse alleyways are packed with Arabian-Nightish colour. Strange heavy odours reach us in the superheated air. Town Arabs sleep on the steps of the Mosque, under luxurious palms, or on the pavement. Burros haul uncanny loads. Veiled Moslem women are indifferent to the impudent whistling. Le Grand Magazin du Globe. Banque de l'Algerie. Our convoy of trucks travels far too quickly and we debouch onto the pinkish plain to the south. Tall eucalyptus trees, thickets of aloe, rows of bearded palm. A tortuous dusty road. Bare hills, like some in southern Alberta. The dust from the convoy envelops us, its neutral taste drying the palate, shutting out the passing scene and irritating the eyes.

Then came the Cork forest and the tent line of No. 1 Canadian Base Reinforcement Depot, British North African Force. No. 1 was a thousand miles from the fighting forces it supported and it had a frightening sense of isolation. Here it was, the last week of September, and Hughes and I displayed a natural concern about our unpredictable future. The Reggio landings had been made on the 3rd, those at Salerno on the 9th. Since then we had been in a vacuum, as far as news was concerned.

*   *   *

Our tent was pitched in a desert of sand, at the edge of the Cork Forest, possibly six hundred feet above the wide reaches of the Mediterranean and two miles from its white beaches. It was hotter than hell fire and we padded about ankle deep in a talc-like dust that rose in clouds with every movement. A full training programme was under way. The valley behind us chattered with small arms fire, the reverberating echoes seeming louder than the weapons themselves. East of us the resounding thump of mortar bombs added a bass note, while in Philippeville direction the pom-pom-pom of Bofors made a noisy background of war-like sound.

In this atmosphere I set about to paint the 2nd Battalion lines, with a background of hills and the distant blue prominence of Cap de Fer. Soon I became aware of a darkening in the sky behind me. Distant Philippeville became enveloped in a cloud that seemed to extend right down to the surface of the sea, resolving itself into a swirling cloud of beige dust, the wall of which I could see slowly advancing toward the encampment. I removed my painting from the easel and tucked it safely into my canvas folio, but before I could get my other equipment packed, the storm struck with unsuspected violence. The first mighty gust carried my easel twenty yards away. I could see tents going down, clothing and laundry rising in convulsive whorls in the enveloping darkness. All was finally obliterated as the storm raged destructively around us for possibly fifteen minutes. When it was over, looking like bin men in a dusty flour mill, we started the search for missing clothing and equipment.

*   *   *

On the third day we were warned, on twenty-four hour notice, for draft. The Permanent Establishment Commander of our Company confided to Hughes and me that a special increment had been created for two historical officers on the first draft out. We were grateful, but when we visited "E" Company orderly room later in the day there was a rumour to the effect that the draft was off indefinitely. Before lights out the rumour was confirmed.

In this atmosphere of uncertainty we continue our tentative existence in the Cork forest. The corners of our mouths and eyes, nostrils and hair-line, have become edged and encrusted with a siliceous deposit, our feet are black when we remove our socks. Dust and heat, they are inescapable except when a bathing parade is authorized. Then we walk the two scorching miles, down through the eroded dunes, to a narrow coastal perimeter of flowering green. We undress on the shell-spangled strand, plunge into the temperate sea, and shout with joy.

*   *   *

A journey offered itself on the tenth day and Hughes and I grasped it, like desperate men. We obtained clearance from the Orderly Room and left early in an open stake bodied truck, turning south through the Arab towns of Danremont and St. Charles, a fertile grape and citrus fruit country. At El Arrouch we topped the rim of a dust bowl depression, which had at its base the canvas city comprising 15th Canadian General Hospital. The tents trembled in the heat and as we approached we sensed the activity, pungent draughts of iodoform reaching us as we drew to a stop to be greeted with quiet western "Hy-yahs"! Here, in an Algerian sandblow, was a Canadian hospital, ministering to the Sicilian casualties. We stopped only long enough to wipe the dust from our faces and wonder how anyone survived the stifling heat.

The country rose gradually, through Wyoming-like hills, supporting a few scattered olive groves. Conde Smendou appeared to contain a concentration of turbanned Arabs, milling about among bleating herds of goats and sheep and squawking domestic poultry. There were no women among them, the young unveiled girls had the palms of their hands stained with henna, a ritual concerned with a religious feast just concluded. In the dusty fields, beyond the town, tilling was being carried out by four-span bullock teams, led by single moth-eaten mules who acted the part of guide like the judas-goat at an abattoir. The ploughboy followed in dangling garments, barely visible in a cloud of dust.

We climbed up, through sagebrush foothills, overtaking an undulating camel caravan with its turbanned outriders, mounted on tiny burros. Then, rounding through a furrow between the arid hills, we reached another plateau, rising from whose floor was the mirage-like butte, on which Constantine stood, thrusting up into the hot atmosphere like some legendary city, an African Lhasa, remote and apart from the modern world. Yet, as we approached in wonder, we could see that we were mistaken. Remarkable structures, in concrete and steel, unfolded and were articulated with the formidable rock formation on which they stood. Tiers of modern mercantile and apartment buildings, suspension bridges and concrete spans, elaborately constructed ramps, tunnels and cuttings, carried the highway approaches into this fabulous city. A spectacular gorge divided the city in two. We parked the truck and entered the nether half, across a suspension foot-bridge which led into the civilized urbanity of a French colonial town.

Our only business in Constantine was to see the place and, if possible, buy a red fez and a bottle of Cognac. We had been warned that eating might be a problem and, being perpetually hungry, our first objective was to find the Municipal Casino and reserve a table there for lunch, which might prove an acceptable variant to the fare at 3rd Battalion Mess. This mission completed, we set about exploring the Rue de France, which appeared to be the main thoroughfare, dividing the Kasbah from the European section. But all efforts to purchase our simple requirements failed, no one seemed to understand French.

Back in the Place de Nemours, the Casino had a movie-set feel about it. Characters appeared, as if for a masquerade: elegant French officers, wearing colourful uniforms under the voluminous burnous, turbanned Moslems, enveloped in Jerds, and a goodly sprinkling of 8th Army types, picturesque in their own bizarre way.

The meal was a revelation. After a glass of Muscatel, a generous serving of diced melon preceded a delicious roasted meat. With the meat was served a bottle of Ben Kala Vin Rouge. The tomato dish was rich with olive oil and strange but attractive spices. Needless to say we were in a good mood to appreciate the fine achievement of French cuisine. The tomatoes were followed by a vast compote of Muscatel grapes and, later, under the sidewalk awning, the almost forgotten joys of crême à là glace were experienced afresh. Before we had finished a demi-tasse of Turkish coffee, a perspiring runner came puffing up with a message from Mr. Roberts, the Auxiliary Services Officer: Would we rejoin the truck immediately? He had orders to return to the Cork forest without delay.

Back in camp, Capt. Smith, our P.E. Company Commander, denied any knowledge of a movement order, looking us straight in the eye saying, "Somebody is talking out of turn. You'll hear in lots of time." At the 3rd Battalion Orderly Room, the staff was silent, but a Corporal handed each of us half a dozen red patches and told us to get them sewn on immediately. This was all the warning we needed. We hurried back to our tent and started to pack. The grape-vine suggested that we were to leave the Cork forest at 1000 hours tomorrow.

It rained steadily and heavily all night. The morning was still, with a troubled sky. But the rain had stopped and the dust had been laid and caked into a firm surface. At breakfast speculation was rife. Knowing the Army as we did, it was agreed that we could not expect more than two hours' notice, but that could come at any minute. How right we were; almost immediately Capt. Smith ordered us to pack and parade

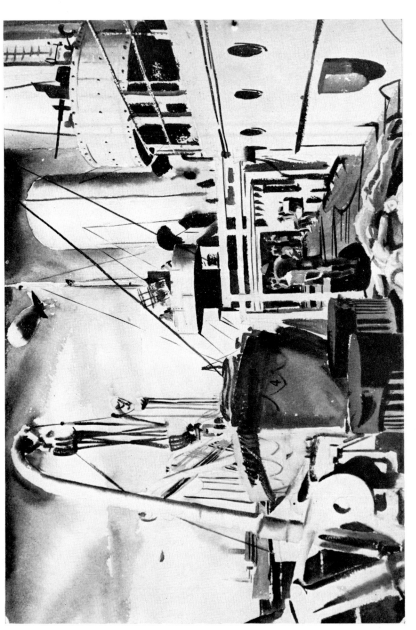

CANADIAN TROOPS ABOARD TRANSPORT *Volendam*. S.S. *California* ON LEFT.

PHILIPPEVILLE, NORTH AFRICA. CAPE DE FER AND STORA BAY IN BACKGROUND.

in front of E. Company Orderly Room at 0930 hours. Everyone paraded punctually, in full marching order. A hot sun
burned through the overcast and blazed down on us as mepa-
crene, water sterilizing tablets, and embarkation cards, were
distributed.

Landing Craft Infantry:

Although we breathed the last of the North African dust, as
we debussed on the quay that morning, its concomitant in the
experience, the blazing sun, was still with us. Someone had
recommended that we would be well advised to wear battle
dress, if the rumour of our sailing in landing craft were
correct. To my great discomfort I had done this and I stood
on the exposed quay at Philippeville, sizzling like a sheep on
a spit. Tars on the Montreal-built frigate, H.M.S. *Cuckmere,*
cool by contrast in tropical white, look on amused. The
rumour had been correct for once: huddled nearby was a
swarm of American L.C.I.'s.

A frowning electric storm sputtered on the western horizon as the frigate *Cuckmere* led her brood out of the harbour.
It was inevitable that the storm would overtake us, since the
convoy speed was relatively slow. Possibly with this in mind,
the O.C. Troops was anxious to get everyone fed, and cook-
house was sounded almost immediately.

Officers and men alike lined up in a single file leading to
the galley service window. Into this window, remotely like
that of a cashier's in a bank, we thrust our mess tins, accepting
the cook's offering with the usual comments. The accommodation on a landing craft is very simple, a place to stand up and
a place to lie down. Mess tins are the dining-room, so having
received one's food it was necessary only to find a place to
stand in order to consume it. The meal was simple but substantial. As we finished, the storm was overhead and the wind
shredded the sea with mighty gusts, whitecaps breaking and
hissing in the gloom alongside.

As the orderly officer and ship's mate shepherded their military charges below, the craft trembled and struggled in the powerful torque of the waves, one moment soaring like a gliding bird over the troubled sea, the next descending with a woeful shudder into great valleys of crackling foam. An L.C.I. displaces 387 tons and draws only 3.5 feet of water, which means that she sits on the surface like an empty shoe box and performs more elaborate convulsions than the latest midway "ride." A thousand dying voices wailed in the ratlines, as the wind roared through the superstructure with the thunder of an express train. Lightning flashes revealed a sea burdened in all directions, with bursting waves veiled in gauzey spume.

Footings becoming treacherous, as seas swept the deck, I retired to the relative safety below. With the dim light turned out, the sleeping quarters glowed cherry-red from the emergency exit markers. Exposed vents, pipes, and stanchions, writhed across the low ceiling in organized confusion, ruddy like great pulsing entrails. A suction vent roared somewhere over my head, trying in vain to expel the fetid odours of hot sweating bodies. In one undivided space, two hundred officers and men were packed in three-tiered layers all about us.

I was on deck at 0620 hours next morning. A confused smoky sunrise with rain squalls all about, and a moderate sea. To port astern was the rocky Ile de Cani, to starboard the sandy hills of Cap Zebib. Hughes and I washed and shaved on deck, in our mess tins, a very serviceable item of equipment. The orderly officer presented the Captain's compliments and informed us that we were invited to breakfast with that officer in his cabin. This was a welcome piece of intelligence. We checked our dress a second time and went below.

Captain White was an affable American who had been a first mate in the Mercantile Marine before the war. "When this fracas is over, I'm gonna grow oranges in the San Bernardino Valley, and never look at a boat again!" He had sailed the No. 218 across the Atlantic, "damn-near broke her in half," and been in all the Mediterranean landings since

November. At Salerno, a Jerry pilot had dropped a torpedo headed right for him. It had passed under the 218 and struck another vessel, two hundred yards beyond.

*   *   *

We are zigzagging continuously. The port tack rolls this tiny vessel considerably, and there is some sickness. Colossal skies, with rain squalls, sweep the sea as we cross the Gulf of Tunis. Immediately ahead of us are the islands of Zembra and Zembretta, impressive rocky peaks, rising hundreds of feet out of the sea. Cap Bon is a rounded foreland, to starboard. Painting is out of the question on this lively craft, but I am making pencil notes of these bold natural features.

At 1445 hours we change course suddenly and Pantelleria can now be seen faintly on the horizon, over the port bow. Here is the ancient route from Carthage to Agrigento and Ostia. Last spring the frantic transports of the retreating axis forces had sailed this course from Sfax to Syracuse. Just three months back the Allied task forces, bound for Sicily, gradually drew together through this sea for their historic rendezvous.

*   *   *

Etna is a mighty silhouette in the west. Above it the mariner's friend, Arcturus, shines with a cold detached jewel-like light. On the summit rests an elongated cloud, like a huge maskinonge. The air is warm and the sea tranquil. We gaze with fascination at this last-light spectacle, with a bright moon, better than half, shining above us.

Capo Passero and Porto Paolo were abeam to port at 1030 hours. We were headed across the Ionian Sea toward the toe of the peninsula. The seas had moderated considerably and I attempted a painting, looking toward the bridge from behind the Oerlikon. The space was very limited and even the long easy swells posed quite a problem. As the ship rolled, my equipment rolled with it.

The cone of Etna was clearly defined now, rising out of the straits to port, having dominated the scene all day. The sea had calmed almost to tranquillity and the air was warmer.

*　　　*　　　*

A school of porpoises plays about the bow, taking an occasional look at us, like shy mermaids, then they are gone. Flying fish, like huge dragon-flies, skim the surface, some of their flights from fifty to sixty yards. The sea is calm and, above the dazzle of the land, a quilted field of clouds hangs motionless. It is a midsummer hot afternoon, as we come to zero speed in Taranto Bay. All day, first the mountainous Calabrian, then the Lucanian coast, has simmered under the blaze.

Of the two hundred aboard our vessel, Canadians numbered one hundred and twenty men and fourteen officers, the balance was largely British. Canadians, in shorts and bushshirts, laughed and talked by the taffrail, drawing tickets in the five shilling "First Line Ashore" lottery. Hughes and I had about us Harry Walker, the cipher officer, Paul Amyot of Signals, Brian Taylor of the Edmontons, and two young lieutenants from the Calgarys—Stafford and Cameron.

We proceeded slowly through the submarine boom gates and closed in on the city as darkness fell. It was a flat, featureless skyline, smudged with smoke and dominated by the keeps of the castle of San Angelo. Signal flags leaped up the Admiralty control staff and an aldus lamp blinked a message to *Cuckmere*. Hard to starboard the dark silhouette of a monitor sat low in the water, backed by a forest of masts and spars. We gazed intently through the miscellaneous shipping, trying to formulate the vague shapes of the darkening city, listening for the first sounds from the shore.

The castle loomed darkly against the evening sky as our column closed in on the entrance to the canal. Shore noises floated out to us. Our passage of the Canale Navigabile was watched by silent groups of Italians. The keeps of San Angelo slipped by and we tied up at the hydroplane jetty in the Mare

Piccolo. The first line went ashore at 1926 hours, and the pool of fifteen pounds went to a young Englishman, Lieut. Radford.

North Through Puglia:

On went the web, the binocular case, the ammunition pouch, the pistol and holster, the haversack, the small pack, the large pack, and then finally, the crushing weight of the bedroll was shouldered. Hughes and I staggered down the landing ramp looking like crumpled cardboard boxes, strangled and garrotted with thongs and straps.

We had spent the night on the L.C.I. and now, at 0815 hours, Oct. 10, 1943, we debarked onto Italian soil. The eleven landing crafts of our convoy had suddenly debouched more than two thousand men on the hydroplane jetty in the Mare Piccolo. We shed our equipment in a picketed area and went off on an inspection tour, pursued by half a dozen child beggars, carrying sacks and shouting demands for "Biscotte" and "Chocolato."

A few hours later, open trucks whisked us quickly through the city. Over the route we took, there was little evidence of its antiquity except for the old castle of San Angelo. With a single tram line, "Arsenale-Ferrovia," it seemed a relatively clean sort of peaches-and-cream coloured town. On empty walls, declamatory statements appeared in bold sans-serif lettering:

Roma E'Veremente il segno fatale della nostra stirpe. Roma non puo essere senza L'Italia, Ma L'Italia non puo'essere senza Roma.

Italian girls discreetly ignored the whistled "wolf calls" issuing from the convoy.

The newer sections of the town displayed no sign of war damage that we could see. In the older city the quays had been heavily bombed and the railway station had received direct hits and was a shambles. But efforts were being made to repair the tracks and there were locomotives about, with steam up, and a considerable amount of undamaged rolling stock.

"VINCERE!"* shouted boldly at us from the walls of an underpass as we left the town. Whose purpose was that to be now?

*   *   *

The Tenuta D'Accetta Grande (the estate of the big hatchet) was an extensive *latifondi* devoted largely to the cultivation of olives and the production of olive oil. The Villino itself was not unattractive, a low rectangular white structure, with a strongly built gateway, giving entrance to a courtyard with a well-head at its centre. It struck me as looking very much like a levantine version of a Hudson's Bay fort, Fort Garry, for instance.

The estate stood high on a great whale-back rise of stony land, offering an impressive view of the Gulf of Taranto. Olive trees, loaded with fruit, climbed and carefully traced every contour of that ancient terrain. Larks filled the sky with song, while great fearsome hornets sampled the corn syrup in my mess tin.

Hughes and I had been assigned a bell-tent with Brian Taylor in a nearby olive grove. We were static again and back on depot routine. No one seemed to know how the battle was going, or where the 1st Canadian Division was. The best information obtainable was that to reach "Main 40" involved a journey of two hundred miles. I had a sponge bath out of a pail of water. As I dried myself a lizard lay pulsing in the hot sun, barely distinguishable from the rock on which it basked.

Our stay at the "Villino" had the recommendation of being brief, fortunately too brief for us to become acquainted with its finer qualities as a base reinforcement depot. In the early morning of the third day we were again loaded into open

---

*"Victory!"

trucks and started on our journey north. A mile or so from the "Villino" we reached a two-lane, black-top highway, not unlike "No. 2" in Ontario, except that the setting was quite different. Our journey took us first across the Salentine peninsula, the southeast corner of the kingdom, often referred to as the "heel of the boot." We climbed around the impressive hill town of Massafra. Just a month before in the public square the Commanding Officer of the 1st Airborne Division had been killed by an enemy sniper. The adult townspeople were sullenly indifferent to our passing, only the children ventured any contact. The Adriatic spread out before us as we topped the height of land at Gioia del Colle. This whole broad coast is packed with interest and here we were, hurtling through it in convoy.

Cassamassima. The grape harvest was going on everywhere. The principal native traffic of the road was concerned with the harvest and with wine. The grapes were contained in large tubs, carried on low wagons. As we passed, bunches were thrown at us, sweet and lush.

*   *   *

I had looked forward to seeing Bari. As we descended on that ancient port, we speculated on what route the convoy might take us through the town.

Phoenicians, Greeks and Romans have left their mark on this city. In the Middle Ages it was the point of contact and departure between the Latin world and the Levant. In the crypt of the cathedral is a Madonna from Constantinople, said to have been painted by St. Luke himself. And then, of course, Frederick, Conrad, and Robert Guiscard have all considered it an important city. There is the legend, too, of the sailors of Bari who forcibly removed the relic of St. Nicholas from its resting place in Myra and brought it home with them where its miraculous powers still impress the faithful.

We were halted to "close up" on a crowded mercantile thoroughfare, known as the Extramurale, down behind the

railway yards, possibly the most squalid and disagreeable location that might have been chosen for a halt. The convoy
officer knew his duties.

At noon we pulled off the road, just beyond San Spirito,
where the highway skirts the bright sea. We debussed and
set to our bully beef and biscuits. An inshore breeze was
delightfully cool and lively breakers crashed on the rocks about
us. Conversation centred about the probable location of the
Division. We knew now that we could not make it that day.
We would sleep in a staging camp for the night. Rumour had
it that the Canadians were with 13th British Corps in the
mountains. None of us had a map, but there was speculative
talk of the Fortore valley, beyond Foggia. We were beginning to realize that we were getting closer now. Doc MacKay
was cheerful but realistic. "We've got no business here,
Comfort. This is a war for young men and old men with no
brains!" As we left the lunch halt, I saw, turning off to the
left, the side road to Bitonto, with one of the richest romanesque treasures in Puglia. It had kept for a long time, it would
have to keep a little longer.

There were half-hearted efforts at merriment in the truck,
as we skirted the sparkling sea with its wonderful beaches.
Except those who were lucky enough to have a seat on the tail-
board or on the baggage, we all stood in the open truck, steady-
ing ourselves with the tarpaulin supports, swaying like strap-
hangers in a crowded street-car. Hughes was in animated
conversation with Stafford and Cameron, on the disposition
and mobility of Hannibal's forces at Cannae. We had
by-passed that ancient battlefield somewhere just north of
Barletta. It was warm in the sun, but the speed of the truck
made a great-coat welcome. Spans of great white oxen
lumbered along the roadside, hauling tubs of grapes to the
wine presses.

The Tavoliere plains are as flat as those in Saskatchewan,
and as fertile, lush and monotonous. As we turned inland,
away from the sea, the blue mountains of Manfredonia were
away to the right. The spidery pilgrim road, reaching up to

the summit of Monte San Angelo could be plainly seen. Legend has it that on that mountain top the Archangel, Michael, made an appearance on earth and revealed himself to St. Lawrence.

We passed a long succession of identical new model farm units. From the heavy stubble in the fields it was apparent that these farms were devoted to intensive grain cultivation. Contact with the following trucks had been lost, so we halted south of Foggia and waited for them to close up.

Foggia is a plains town, somewhat larger than Regina and with a considerably longer history. It is strategically situated, and the surrounding flat terrain makes it an ideal location for military airfields protecting south-central Italy. One of the primary Allied objectives, at the time of the continental landings, had been to deny the enemy the use of these fields and secure them for ourselves. The town, being a communications and supply centre had, of military necessity, been bombed. What we saw was devastation and, since the bombing had occurred only a short time earlier, little had yet been done to tidy up the mess. Other than the harbour bombings at Taranto, this was the first really destructive war damage we had seen in Italy. Now that the Allied air forces were using these bases, the Luftwaffe paid occasional sudden sharp visits, so that Foggia was having her hair parted on both sides and down the middle as well. We rolled through on a marked route, breathing the smells of burned lumber, privies, and damp old plaster. Out on the plains again we continued, with growing hunger and weariness, increasingly indifferent to the site of the staging camp.

*   *   *

The staging camp was in an olive grove a mile outside Lucera. I slept in the open, under a full moon that belied our mission. Toward morning it became chilly and a heavy dew hung on the mosquito net. We stirred as a pale dawn grew in the east, and after hurried ablutions and a makeshift breakfast, were marshalled into the trucks. Our route skirted the

town and brought us almost immediately under the battlements
of Frederick's castle. As we lurched up the uneven road,
Hughes peered intently through his glasses at the ancient
masonry, as if reading some forgotten legend in its textures.

How well the stronghold fitted into the flat terrain. It had
that quality of belonging, almost like a Frank Lloyd Wright
structure. The town receded and evidences of the modern
battle grew as we approached the mountains. Tracks of
armour scarred the foothills, artillery and mortar ammunition
stood in abandoned stacks. Demolitions, and their attendant
diversions, became more frequent. And then there were the
graves of the newly dead. The dual trails of armour and
tracked vehicles were graven into the hillsides, as if incised
by some meticulous draughtsman, tracing the movements of a
vast mechanized game of hide-and-seek. We were getting
closer, and so were the mountains. As we climbed the rising
gradients and made the hairpin turns, the plain fell away below
us. Lucera disappeared in the distance and Monte Gargano
became a faint silhouette.

Stafford and Taylor were hospitalized Sicilian casualties,
returning to their units. They too were animated with the
excitement that filled us all. Our route lay over precipitous
curving roads, a continuously mountainous country in vast
contrast to yesterday's pancake plains and the rolling plateau
of the Murge. The crowding peaks about us recalled the
Cascades, or the Selkirks, in their wild rugged impressiveness.

We descended in a long series of hairpin turns to the spectacular Fortore crossing. Two arches of the great masonry
bridge had been blown, and the diversion ford was carefully
taped for mines. We bobbled across and had lunch with
elements of Rear Div. in the valley beyond.

Shortly after leaving Gambatesa, we heard gunfire for the
first time. It sounded a long way off, a dull muffled tocsin that
set the heart thumping. The chatter died down in the truck
and there was silence, except for the noise made by the vehicle
itself. We all listened intently as another distant salvo echoed
through the hills.

At 1615 hours we turned off the road near Riccia, and
ascended a steep stony grade to a huddle of ill-kept farm
buildings. We were at Main 40, Headquarters 1st Canadian
Infantry Division.

*   *   *

The Camp Commandant did not know where the Historical Section was. Capt. Thrupp, in the "I" lorry, pointed
vaguely across a glade, toward a wood on a forward slope.

Eventually we found an ageing Humber staff car that had
come all the way from El Alemein and looked it. Against one
side, a rough tarpaulin lean-to barely covered the belongings
that lay beneath it. A rough sign, stuck in the ground, said
"Hist. Sec." We had arrived.

No one was about so we sat down and tried to feel at
home. There was some satisfaction in having completed the
approach phase of our mission without incident and we were
rather pleased with ourselves. The mediums in the field
beyond the wood barked with an angry vigour.

As darkness fell, we were directed to a battered F.O. tent,
identified as "E" mess. As I stooped to enter, a familiar
voice said "No strangers allowed in this mess. . . ." It was
my life-long friend, Will Ogilvie. Up to that time Hughes
had been my constant companion, and although we were still
to share the vicissitudes of the Italian campaign together for
a year, we realized that the individual character of our duties
would often separate us. On the other hand, my arrival at the
Division brought me in close contact once more with Ogilvie,
whom I had last seen in London in April, when we dined
together at a Jermyn Street restaurant with Allison Grant and
Kay Moore. Since then he had taken part in the Sicilian landings and followed the fortunes of the Division to this point.
After being introduced to the P.M.C., Capt. "Bill" Hall,
M.C., and Capt. A. T. "Gus" Sesia, the Historical Officer, we
sat down to a noisy meal in almost complete darkness. Talking
never ceased.

After the meal, we returned to the Section lean-to where Ogilvie dug around in his dunnage bag and produced, from the folds of a suit of heavy underwear, a bottle of Kummel, liberated in Sicily and carefully nursed for just this occasion. In the company of Hughes and Sesia, and loud military noises in the next field, we ceremoniously opened the bottle. Appropriate toasts were proposed and then we continued with the serious business of reviewing the crowded events that were now part of all our lives.

PART

II

THE CAMPAIGN

Campobasso:

> Vor der Kaserne, vor dem grossen tor
> Stand eine laterne un steht sie noch davor.
> So wall'n wir uns da wiederseh'n
> Bei der laterne woll'n wir steh'n
> Wie einst Lili Marlene, wie einst Lili Marlene.

As we clattered over the railway tracks at the southern entrance to the town, citizens were crouching behind walls and sheltering in doorways. Then came a sudden screaming, ear-splitting CRUMP, a wall tottered outward and disintegrated as it fell into the street, enveloped in a choking pall of fine dust. An artificial hush fell on the scene, a sort of reflex silence following the blast. Now we too were sheltering in what cover the situation afforded. The collective thinking of the group could be felt, was almost audible: Would there be another? The dust was redolent of fire and ageing plaster. As it cleared, a truck approached, lurching through the fallen masonry. In it we saw a group of gesticulating civilians, huddled about three enemy soldiers. They edged over to where we stood and complained that their prisoners had been sniping at non-combatants. Another shell arched overhead with a shrill phantom-like whine. We all ducked, prisoners as well. The explosion shook the neighbourhood but did us no harm. The enemy soldiers denied the civilian charges, their principal spokesman looking calmly at Cottam through thickish glasses. They had, however, carelessly forgotten to dispose of their pay-books, and after confirming the fact that they were Panzer Grenadiers, Cottam directed the truck to the P.O.W. cage and we made our way into Campobasso.

*   *   *

The Gildone road had not yet been swept for mines, so that on leaving the Division that morning we first sped south on a detour through the narrow cobbled streets of Riccia. The windshield was strapped down over the engine hood and covered against glare, producing all the sensations of flying in an open-cockpit plane. The chill wind tore at clothing and penetrated beneath to my shivering body. But I was too concerned with hanging on to the careening jeep itself to remedy the situation. The countryside was magnificent under a field of a great feather-bed nimbus. Near Decorata it had the nobility and grandeur of the Scottish highlands. The Matese massif, dominated by the lofty peak of Miletto, was the background.

We reached Brigade conveniently around lunch time and were hospitably greeted and fed at the roadside by a smiling, moustached Seaforth, Captain Norman Pope. A nearby battery shattered the sunlit day with violent salvos punctuating Cottam's interrogation of two prisoners and adding a nervous quality to our pencil sketches.

On this delightful and exciting occasion Ogilvie and I had accepted the invitation to accompany Capt. Cottam on an "I"

recce (Intelligence reconnaissance). Since we had no transportation of our own, his thoughtfulness provided us with the
opportunity to acquire facts and colour concerning the activities of the Division which might otherwise have been missed.
Kenneth Cottam was a remarkable, if reckless, Yorkshireman,
attached to our "I" staff. He had a youthful Tudor appearance, a boisterous sense of humour, a matchless digestion, and
the courage of a lion.

At the Anti-Tk. command post, Major Arthur "Tiger"
Welch, just in from up front, said that our troops were already
in Campobasso and that Kesselring's boys were throwing lots
of stuff back into the town. Cottam was impatient. "Come
on, let's go!" Campobasso was several difficult miles away,
but we were on our way immediately.

The shelling was continuous but not heavy. Cottam wanted
to interview the Podesta, if such there was and if he could be
located. We were interested. At the Municipio we were
effusively greeted by an immaculately polished officer of the
Carabinière. We ourselves were covered in dust from head
to foot and, by contrast, presented a rather desperate appearance. Chairs were proffered and declined; a civilian official
assured us that everything was being done to locate the
Podesta, an assurance we did not take too seriously. The
Podesta could not be found. We had guessed that he might
consider it more prudent to remain undiscovered, but we were
in no position to enforce his appearance and withdrew on pre-
text of more urgent duties elsewhere. Cottam had already
obtained a considerable fund of information, both official and
private.

Back in the streets, civilians appeared more confident and
inquisitive, quite a number were standing about our jeep discussing its construction. Shop fronts and lower windows, however, remained tightly shuttered and barred. Red, white and
green Italian flags were appearing draped from balconies, and
an occasional amusing home-made Union Jack could be seen.
We toured the streets, empty of vehicular traffic. Shells were
still coming in at the rate of about one a minute. Our survey

showed that the grist mill had been destroyed, the railway
station badly hit, and the round-house a shambles of twisted
girders. Into the firebox of each of the five steam locomotives
the enemy sappers had placed a demolition charge, which had
effectively ended their usefulness. There were no lights, no
telephones, no power; the pumping station had been demolished. Otherwise, Campobasso was in fairly presentable
shape. We returned to Divisional H.Q. in the darkness,
exhausted and blue with cold. I had spent my first day with
Canadian troops in Italy.

*   *   *

Our arrival at 1st Div. H.Q. heralded a long and varied
association with the town and countryside around Campobasso.

High in the eastern foothills of the Appenines, Campobasso is the provincial capital of the Molise. The modern city,
comparable in size to Lethbridge, or Galt, sits proudly apart
from the older town, crowded around the base of the formidable castle rock. A winding road leads to the 16th century
Castello Monforte, from the battlements of which a sweeping
view of the Matese and the rolling foothills country may be
had.

Following the Canadian occupation of Campobasso, Divisional Headquarters moved forward to the dubious shelter of
a holm-oak wood in rolling farm lands, three miles south of the
town. Hist. Sec. set up its tarpaulin shelter beside an ancient
sheep track or drove road. These drove roads have been used
by the shepherds of Puglia and the Abruzzi since time
immemorial. Our sheep track was a lesser one, *traturelli;*
about the width of St. Catherine Street, it had somewhat the
appearance of a dried-up river bed over which grass has
grown. Centuries of use had pounded it well below the level
of the adjoining fields, like an English lane. Beside this road,
Hughes wrote his reports, while Ogilvie and I completed water
colour painting started further afield,

One morning the G.2, Major Trumbull Warren, visited our shelter. He had an idea: Campobasso had been made a rest centre and re-christened "Maple Leaf City"; why not put on an exhibition of war paintings there for all ranks to see? It might provide a lot of interest and keep the boys out of the bars! Though we had no illusions about the latter suggestion, we did agree that such a project might prove an interesting feature in a rest centre.

An hour later a runner appeared—the G.S.O.1, Colonel Harding, would like to see us and our work. He received us in his caravan with the official formality of a busy officer. He looked and listened with composed interest and while enthusiastic about what he saw, we never knew whether we had been wise in pointing out to him our need for transportation and shelter. Two hours later, Lieut. Marshal Stearns presented the General's compliments and requested that Ogilvie and I present ourselves immediately with our work. Major-General Guy Simonds was most cordial, looked carefully at the paintings and drawings with enthusiasm and expressed his personal interest in our programme.

*   *   *

Whether through coincidence or not, the day following our interview with the Divisional Commander a 15 cwt. was placed at the disposal of Hist. Sec. Ogilvie had been impatient operating from Division, if for no other reason than the fact that Main 40 was smothered in a valley and removed from the action we knew to be going on. We had both looked upon Ferrazzano, high on its conical hill, as a possible viewpoint from where we might see and make drawings of the terrain over which the Division was fighting. Cesia and Hughes now agreed to get us there immediately.

Ferrazzano is a grey-haired little hill village that attracts and repels at one and the same time. Viewed from the valley, it has the romantic appearance of a miniature Monte St.

Michele; within its enclosing walls, it betrays all the sordid evidences of crowding poverty. Its narrow alleys wind round the hill in a logarithmic spiral toward a surprisingly airy piazza at its summit. On one side of the piazza stands what may once have been a princely villa, known to us as the *Casa*. Then there is an anonymous parish church with a Venetian campanile and a severe looking building which might have been a seminary. "A" Company of the 48th Highlanders of Canada held the location at the time and, lord of all he surveyed, was the 2 i/c of that Company, the handsome and picturesque Captain Hamish MacIntosh. The only smiles we saw in Ferrazzano were on the faces of villagers, particularly the age-ing female villagers, who followed the swing of Captain Mac-Intosh's kilt as he led us to his Headquarters. For them he was undoubtedly one of the "ladies from hell." I subsequently made a water colour sketch of him, seated in his headquarters as Hughes interviewed him for a report on the Company's battle experiences. It is not a great painting, but I think it catches some of the congested atmosphere of that little room in Ferrazzano, and contains some evidence of the Captain's hospitality.

With Captain MacIntosh's permission, Ogilvie and I set up a temporary studio in the "Casa." We found George Damar there, with an artillery "O-pip" (observation post) set up in an attic room, picking up targets and reporting the result of fire to a command post of the 1st Field Regiment. The location suited both our purposes. Although we were conscious of the possibility of an O-pip drawing enemy fire, we all agreed that each passing hour lessened that possibility. The fighting we knew was somewhere in the vicinity of Colle d'Anchise and Baranello; smudges of grey smoke rose into the clear air in that direction. We looked out over the texture of roof tiles, embroidered at the edges with heavy stones. Each curving cobbled street was a deep canyon, hidden in shadow. Beyond the walls lay the valley, below us was the tiny village of Mirabello Sannitico, opposite, to the west, the bare contours of the La Rocca feature hid the wooded foothills of the Matese.

Here was the terrain our Division was fighting over; as such it became the valid subject of our interest. I mustered my equipment and set about painting the La Rocca feature, while Ogilvie worked on a distant view of Campobasso from another vantage point.

I looked out over the rolling terrain of a monumental landscape, gradually relating its heaving contours on the paper before me. It was a scene of serene and composed beauty which, paradoxically enough, concealed the savagery of the battle proceeding from every inch of cover offered. Not a man or a gun was to be seen, yet the rolling thunder of artillery never ceased for a moment. An impressive formation of twenty-four Kittyhawks roared overhead, veered west, and then, unchallenged by the Luftwaffe, dive-bombed and strafed enemy positions less than a mile away. Almost before the dust and smoke had cleared, two Jerry reconnaissance planes passed over at great height in clouds of flak.

About this time we noticed the 48th moving forward out of the village in single file, and an hour later George Damar dismantled his O-pip and followed them. This was the last we saw of Damar. Three weeks later we learned that he had been killed. This was the tragic pattern, repeated with depressing regularity through the whole experience, one established contacts with gay, spirited young men, saw and admired them briefly, and then learned the worst.

Ogilvie and I were now the sole garrison at Ferrazzano. Accepting this new role with the leisurely interest of despots ruling a vassal state, we decided to reconnoitre the town afresh. Ogilvie undertook a personal and unattended progress in an ambitious attempt to barter "M and V" for such other commodities as were lacking in our ration box. Half an hour later he returned exultant with two litres of vino bianca and nine priceless candles, a hopeful indication of hidden resources. Furthermore he had contacted one Professore Albino who had agreed to bring us eggs, fruit, and more vino that evening. We were beginning to regret the fact that we were to be picked up next day and the dilapidated salons of the "Casa" took on a new and convincing enchantment. Nightfall brought the Professore and he was as good as his word. We did not detain him and, having delivered his trade goods, he showed no inclination to remain.

A memorable night followed to the noisy and spectacular accompaniment of fire and sound from gun sites in the valleys around us. We had our meal on an outside balcony, surrounded by a delightful ironwork balustrade and overhung by the spreading branches of an ancient fig tree. Below us the darkened landscape was alive with sudden jets of muzzle-flash and the hills echoed with diatonic sound. Mellowed, and indifferent to what went on about us I read aloud to Ogilvie, by candlelight my most recent letters from Louise and A. Y. Jackson.

*   *   *

Back at the Division the weather was like a long and delightful extension of summer. Ken Cottam had a parade of German prisoners drawn up in two ranks on the drove road. Having been told to empty their pockets on the ground in front of them, an odd assortment of schoolboy possessions appeared. They were then directed to pick up their hats, handkerchiefs, any food and personal articles, and were marched off, leaving the remainder for examination.

Ogilvie and I lost no time in arranging another attachment; I planned to go to the 2nd Field Regiment, Ogilvie to the Three Rivers Tanks. There was a general feeling of optimism around the camp and an impatience to get on with the next phase of the battle. Colonel Harding lent me a bivy, less the necessary supports, for which I was extremely grateful. I could easily cut the supports from the nearest cane brake and I would now be independent as far as shelter was concerned.

*   *   *

My first night with 10th Battery was an uncomfortable one. The ground I had bedded down on was more than a little rough and sloped from head to foot. First light found the location shrouded in a heavy mist and everything wringing wet. Crammed into my bivy with kit and equipment, I was stiff, sore, wet and hungry. Pasquale, the Major's driver, came to ask for my mess tin and before I had my shoes laced, he was back with beans, sausage-meat, bread and tea. In spite of the discomfort, it had been an easy night. There had been occasional shoots, but nothing of consequence. Shortly after seven, "Take Post" ended the meal and the misty tranquillity of the morning was shattered by a six-minute shoot. . . . The sun rose, the mists dispersed, and we hung out our clothing and equipment to dry.

*   *   *

At sixteen forty hours, when dusk is settling, an order is passed: We are to be on our way in twenty minutes. Supper has been forgotten in the urgency of the movement. At seventeen hundred we stand ready for the signal. A chill darkness falls, hunger grows, we wait, unable to move from beside the vehicles. An hour . . . two hours . . . pass. The enterprising among us brew tea, as unseen traffic moves constantly on the Biferno road. At nineteen-thirty the signal comes and we move out gingerly onto the road behind two Despatch Riders. I ride in the cab of Major Kingston's vehicle. As soon as we are assembled, the convoy moves off into utter and complete darkness except for a faint glimmer of light on the differential of the jeep preceding. Once over the crest and on the forward slope of the hill we are subject to enemy observation. A hooded flashlight directs us around a gaping hole on the verge of the road and, as we edge round it, we are conscious of a deep valley below us. Jagged unprotected tears in the roadway occur frequently, convincing evidence that the road has been under fire. After many halts and two hours later, an unseen guide directs us off the road, up a steep incline, through a stubble field, to a wooded crest, where we hide the limbers, site the guns, and at last set up our bivies in the blackness.

*   *   *

It was a restless noisy night. I did not dare take off my shoes. Hardly had I stretched out on the uneven ground when the cry of "Take Post!" reached me over the other battle noises. Battery target . . . link control . . . ten-nine-fifty . . . five rounds . . . charge three. Then the shattering roar on the command "Fire!" I lay in my greatcoat, hands clasped under my head, trying to articulate thoughts amid the din. There was no possibility of sleep. Hunger and physical discomforts were of no concern. Violent sound had been normal to this experience for two weeks now and adjustment was taking place. A tolerance did develop; in fact one felt supremely alive and aware. . . . The last round echoes in the darkness; I had the sensibility that we were in a valley, surrounded by hills. I walked over to the Command Post. The duty officer did not think we would get much rest. Enemy mortars were holding up an Infantry advance near Torella del Sannio and it was partly our task to turf them out. His prediction came true; a truly noisy restless night.

Morning disclosed our position: we were sited in a field below the town of Oratino, a beautiful location. The town was high on a ridge above us. To reach our targets there was barely clearance above its tiled roofs and chimneys. There was something about the town that reminded me of Edinburgh Castle. It was built on a high rocky spur, jutting out into the magnificent Biferno valley. Two strong flights of Mitchells passed over; we heard the distant thuds and saw a pall of smoke rising in the direction of the hidden town of Frosinone. The advice was that we were to stand by in readiness to move on a moment's notice. This restricted my activities considerably and I confined my work to brief sketches.

The day was as busy and noisy as the night. The Biferno River below us was a troublesome obstacle. It is a wooded, hill-enclosed valley not unlike parts of the upper Gatineau. The enemy sappers had done an excellent job of demolition on the bridge leading to Castropignano, and, in addition, had successfully mined every usable ford and probable diversion. Their efficiency, combined with the flood-water condition of the river itself, confronted us with a major task in supplying our forces already on the other side. While our mine-clearance operation was under way, the enemy had the locations taped and raked our Engineers constantly with heavy mortar fire.

Just as night was closing in on us again, the familiar "Take Post!" was bellowed from the command post, as it had been all day. Stand by for an "Uncle" barrage, eighty-one rounds, charge three. There was a murmuring stir as the Sergeants checked their ammo and charges. An "Uncle" barrage is a Divisional shoot, every available gun was to fire eighty-one rounds, sounding like support for a "last light" Infantry attack. The first fifteen minutes would be a concentration, the second a timed creeping barrage.

I selected a vantage point and waited for the order. At 1730 hours, in the almost complete darkness, the night was cracked open with fire and super thunder. Never had I heard or seen such infernal theatre. There were moments of continuous arc-like brightness under the black sky. Oratino, on its crag, was side-lit like Klingsor's castle in a Gordon Craig setting. At one instant the image of its sky-line registered black on the retina, the next it was white like a photographic negative. The valley seemed like a garden of blinding flamejets, rocked by the deafening volcanic crashes of creation. The muzzle-brake on the guns split the flame of the burning propellant into long fiery tridents, blue-white tongues of flame. This indeed was the mad, reckless energy of war . . . a percussion cacophony of death that outstripped any other audible experience. The gunners worked like demon puppets, no word of command passing between them, only a continuous dance of galvanic action. Passing ammunition . . . locking and opening the breach . . . ramming home the charge . . . jerking the trigger lanyard . . . all done in the dark or by the flash of neighbouring guns. No language sacred or profane had power or force in the situation. Command Post officers watched every movement. The command had been given; there was nothing to do but wait for it to be carried to its completion. . . . At 1800 hours, as suddenly as it started, the violence ended. The

de profundis silence which followed was like a numbed vacuum,
the sort of dark sepulchral silence that must have preceded the
happenings in Genesis. But gradually distant voices swam into
the field of consciousness again. Gunners laughed and lit
cigarettes. Sergeants counted spent shell cases and reported
expenditures. The "Uncle" shoot was over.

*   *   *

Back by the drove road, the rainy season seemed suddenly
to set in, day after day of drizzle. Officers and men, wearing
all the clothing they possessed, mud to the knees, huddled
about small charcoal fires, made in biscuit tins or oil cans. In
our improvised lean-to, we felt that the limit for existence had
been reached. Bedrolls and blankets were wet, even ground-
sheets and gas-capes failed to keep them dry. Ogilvie struggled
hopelessly with the drainage. There was little to do but "get
used to it," as the song advises.

On one of these depressing days, Jerry Mudge appeared
with jeep and driver, with which we were deeply impressed.
I had not seen Mudge since the Cork Forest, Ogilvie had
never met him.

Mudge wanted to know if Ogilvie and I would take the
rest cure with him and Captain Batty at the "Royal York" in
Campobasso that evening. We needed very little coaxing as
we had heard much of how Captain Forbes Thrasher had
transformed the Albergo Grande for the entertainment of
Canadians. The hotel was a modest little one on the Via
Veneto. Any discrepancy in size between it and its Toronto
namesake was fully compensated for by the intensity with
which life was lived within its walls. Thrasher had done an
admirable job, received his guests personally, and there was a
friendliness reminiscent of the Lord Nelson in Halifax. The
dining-room was small and the cuisine limited to the raw
materials of Army rations but, as was often the case, a good
Italian chef had converted these familiar staples into dishes
of extraordinary attractiveness. What a little garlic, pimento,

or chopped onion, will do to Bully is unbelievable. Then, of course, there were wines, not the famous labels from Montefiascone or Frascati, but the stronger vintages of the east coast region, bracketed under the general heading of Vino.

The atmosphere of the dining-room was stifling as an ageing *camerière* bowed us to a reserved table. The place was crowded with perspiring khaki-clad officers from every unit in the Division. On a raised platform in a corner, almost hidden by potted palms and a dense fog of tobacco smoke, was a four-piece orchestra languidly playing Santa Lucia. White wine was served immediately, referred to as Asti-Spumante, though many of us knew differently. Lieut. Wray, another young Mounted Policeman, joined us, making with Mudge and Batty a rather formidable Provost escort. Our acquaintances raised their eyebrows and could hardly be blamed for thinking that we must be under open arrest. Of what possible misdemeanour could such innocent characters be guilty?

With a stern-looking elderly man seated immediately beside her, a plump young woman sat just a little apart from the orchestra. The disparity in their ages made them a conspicuously odd pair. The girl seemed nervous and fanned herself constantly. It soon transpired that she was the contralto soloist about whom we had heard so much, and the alert elderly gentleman was her father, who sat all evening guarding his treasure. Under the circumstances, this old Italian custom seemed a very wise precaution.

Spirits rose with the temperature of the room and under the stimulus of lashings of vino bianca. Shrill greetings mingled with oblique epithets, and I remember that someone sang quite well. This proved only the beginning. Major Cromb and three fellow officers from the Edmontons provoked roars of laughter, and other hilarious critical noises when they attempted to sing the quartette from "Rigoletto." Following this tempestuous interlude, the contralto rose from her chair, handed a colourful shawl to papa, and advanced to the front of the platform with a frightened little smile. A deafening round of applause greeted her appearance. She bowed, smiled a little more confidently, and then waited patiently for the hand-clapping and whistling to subside before nodding to the orchestra.   The cello throbbed with the opening bars of Schubert's "Ave Maria," a respectful hush fell over the room, then the rich warm voice reached into the prayer with devastating tremolo.

As she swayed emotionally, with clasped hands, one could have heard a pin drop.   Handkerchiefs appeared, noses were blown, throats cleared.   The emotional strain was too great. Fatigue, the unaccustomed heat, the vino, Schubert, the cello, the contralto, combined to dissolve many a brave soldier into tears, before the final trembling note faded and was consumed in thunderous applause.   The entertainment deteriorated rapidly, following this climactic performance, into a sort of deafening riot of "Barber Shop" harmony.   We left the "Royal York" before the evening had reached its full-blown maturity.   We had had the rest cure.

At Main 40 it rained in earnest and was inhospitably cold. Sitting still in the open to paint, returning cold and wet to an open tarpaulin shelter, without light or heat, I found it increasingly difficult to do my work.   The best resolutions bogged down in absolute misery.   It was about this time that Capt. Cesia informed us that he was being returned to England, and was leaving to embark at Naples the following day. It was necessary for an officer to be with the vehicle on the return journey and I was delighted to be chosen to accompany him.

Naples, November:

> O dolce Napoli
> O suol beato!

We had come from the very centre of the Molese, but, in spite of uncounted diversions, we had made excellent time.

At Capodichino, we joined the heavy traffic from the 5th Army front, and shortly reached the high ridge that marks

the northern limits of Naples.   There was the teeming city, the
city of San Gennaro and, beyond it, that amphitheatre of timeless beauty.   High in the air swung the balloon barrage, pointing into the wind.   The harbour was crowded with martial
shipping, L.C.T.'s, transports, lighters, freighters and ships of
war, in great variety.   We hesitated a moment before swinging onto the curving descent to the Via Foria.

Vesuvius dominated the scene, with a sprawl of white villas
tumbling down and thickening, as they approached the Autostrada, and the beaches of Torre del Greco and Ercolano.
Capri was a hazy silhouette in a shimmering sea, with the blue
ridges of the Sorrento peninsula beyond.

The bay disappeared and we found ourselves on the Corsa
Garibaldi, approaching the station.   I was impressed with the
busy normality of the place.   The Centrale Station stood
intact, with its arcaded façade, and carefully pruned plane trees.
The Corso Umberto Primo had not escaped so easily, however.   The Albergo Napoli, where I had stayed on my last
peacetime visit, was a deserted ruin, Dr. Bassler's room, where
we had discussed his ascent of Etna, having been shorn in
half, lay bare to the weather.   Oleander trees were broken
and twisted, the Church of San Pietro di Martire a scorched
shell, not unlike St. Clement's Dane in the Strand. Royal palms
were mutilated, their finery hanging limply or wilted in the
gutter.   Twisted piles of rusting wire filled former flower beds
with angry barbs.

We crossed on San Felice and passed the blackened remains
of Santa Chiara.   I was saddened that its glory had gone and
that its calcined walls contained only the debris of that supreme
example of baroque magnificence and the Gothic tomb of
Robert the Wise.   I remembered the almost carnival grandeur
of Del Gaizo's decor, and those joyous anthems of moving
colour in the ceiling by Francesco di Mura.   Now it was gone,
the accretion of seven centuries of artistic development consumed by fire bombs in one night.

On the Via Tarsia, the Town Major gave us chits on the
Albergo Patria, the Allied Officers' Transit Camp.   Fiddler

dropped Sesia and me there, taking the Humber off to the picketed area up on Capodimonte.

Crowded with officers of all the Allied armies, the Patria had a cosmopolitan atmosphere. The foyer echoed with masculine conversation, like the convention floor of perhaps the Mount Royal, front-line experiences, amorous triumphs, last night's sharp Luftwaffe raid, the rising price of wines and liquors. We were assigned an elegant room, with twin beds, for twenty lire each per day. I felt almost a sense of guilt, when I contrasted the gaudy luxury of room seventy-nine with the slit-trenches and bivies I had left on the Biferno.

Next morning at A.F.H.Q. we found that Capt. Sesia's embarkation would be delayed for a day or two, and we decided that we would attempt an ascent of Vesuvius, on the King's time, and in the King's vehicle, before I returned to Division.

At Ercolano, we turned north through Resina and ascended the low outer slope of the mountain over a dreadful road that had known no repair for years. Climbing steeply between high walls, which hid the pink soil and the lush vineyards, it was only at the frequent hairpin turns that one saw the Bay spreading out below. Before reaching the Observatory, we stopped at a nameless ristorante and cajoled the proprietor into preparing a lunch for us, to be ready on our return.

Up we went, past the Observatory, recalling Palmiere and the eruption of 1872, which had swept around that point. Walls and vegetation disappeared. As we climbed through a barren waste of old lava, the road became rougher, and then became simply a track, over comparatively new flows. Finally our progress was obstructed by a flow which crossed the track and was possibly forty feet high.

Here, we left the Humber with Fiddler and engaged one of two elderly Italian guides who were waiting at this strategic point. We were now well within the Atrio d'Cavallo. Tacking back and forth, up a steep gravelly slope, before getting onto the new lava flow which, we were informed, had occurred in the past year, the climbing was pleasant and the view stupendous. We then topped a ridge and entered the Valle dell'Inferno, acres of twisted flinty lava, like a gargantuan spill of toffee. Here and there were hot fumerole, steaming and smelling strongly of sulphur. Out of the middle of this rose the central cone, a shaley rock pile, at the top of which was the vent, emitting the exhaust, which rose fifty feet in a steady white column before breaking into a voluminous, billowing white cloud which hung above the summit of the mountain.

As we approached the cone, we could hear menacing subterranean rumbles, like distant gunfire. Following each disturbance, a colossal splash of molten magma rose into the air and, because of the scale of the scene, descended onto the cone with the visual effect of slow-motion photography. At the base of the cone, as we halted to rest and observe, a boy appeared from nowhere and miraculously produced an oversize bottle of wine. We were not consulted as to our wishes but simply passed a large glass of wine and later asked to pay for it. We appreciated both the wine and the excellent timing of its appearance, which added much to our appreciation of the awesome spectacle. Another youth, inviting coins from us, proceeded up the cone to the vent and then, as a shower of magma gouted out, plunged the coin into it and, returning, sold it back to us, weaklings that we were.

The descent was rapid and spectacular and provided a greater opportunity for looking about us. The new lava flows were suggestive of massive sculptural form. Every development of animal life since the trilobite seemed to struggle for identity in the muscular contours that flexed and extended themselves in all directions. Climbing over the lip of the modern crater, one looked down over a tumbling moraine into the fearsome depths of the Atrio d'Cavallo on the one hand, and out over the devastating beauty of the great Bay on the other. It was a day of hazy warm sunshine which contributed much to a sense of creative wonder evoked by this moving sight. I swept the Bay, from the promontory of Posillipo to Castellammare, quietly reflecting on the peaceful images of classic beauty which succeeded one another and each feature took shape and released its burden of recollection. The war seemed far away indeed.

We found Fiddler and the Humber without much difficulty, and shortly after one o'clock were back at the ristorante. Lunch was served *al fresco* under vines on a high arboured terrace overlooking the Bay. Besides the unforgettable prospect, the slope of Vesuvius contributed the wine, a memorable roseate vintage, known as Lachryma Christi. Inspired by the scene, we paraded the dramatis personae of the area, from Virgil to Benedetto Croce, with special consideration for interim visitors and residents, such as Goethe and Joseph Mallord William Turner. From my point of view, the ascent of Vesuvius had been a great success.

Next morning I said good-bye to Captain Sesia and Fiddler and I left him to embark, when a ship was available, while we returned to the Division.

Campobasso II:

Naples had been bathed in warm sunshine; the Biferno front had had continuous rains and quaking cold. Life by the drove road had not improved in our absence, in fact the drove road had become a torrent and the approaches to the camp site were axle-deep in yellow mud. We harboured the vehicle and sought out the dreary shelter of our sagging tarpaulin. Hughes and Ogilvie returned muddy and white-faced from Torella, where they had lain in a shallow ditch, trapped by shell and mortar fire. Hughes paced up and down, sucking at his pipe, recounting the experience which, I gathered, had been extremely uncomfortable.

Ogilvie had had a visitor in my absence. Major Dick Malone, Q.O.R., had dropped in from Army, presented General Montgomery's compliments and requested that we bring the entire exhibition of paintings which we proposed to show in Campobasso to the General's Headquarters at Vasto. Accommodation had been assigned for the purpose at the Beaver Club and Provosts had been detailed to picket the show and regulate the crowds, if they materalized. We had made a selection from the paintings available and gone to elaborate pains to mount them on white matts salvaged from the local Casa del Fascio.

On a wet cheerless morning in early November, Ogilvie and I picked up our four-man Provost guard at the Ops. tent and headed for Campobasso in the Humber. At the Beaver Club we posted our guards and opened the first exhibition of painting ever to be offered for the enjoyment of fighting men in a theatre of war and within sound of battle. The Beaver Club had been set up in a smart new Fascist Youth Recreation centre. We had been assigned a large room with good north-east light and around the walls we hung fifty-four paintings.

The Club was crowded with troops that morning and to our delighted surprise when the doors of the exhibition were unceremoniously opened, they did not wander in by twos and threes, but simply surged in in a great mob. The hours during which the paintings could be viewed were determined by the light of day. We had no way of blacking out the windows and at any rate there was insufficient power to provide artificial light. The paintings were all field sketches in water colour, covering the Sicilian and Italian campaigns up to that date, and it was gratifying to us to see knots of men assembled about the paintings and carrying on animated discussions, recalling personal experiences at a particular location, and discussing the merit of the work. All displayed enthusiastic interest in the project and, at the end of the two days on which the exhibition was open, the Provost count showed that 3,137 Canadian soldiers of all ranks had visited it. We were gratified, and so was Major Warren.

*   *   *

The wind-swept hill country east of Campobasso had a melancholy bleakness, perhaps accentuated by the weather and

the circumstances of war. Great treeless undulations over
which the road winds, now in a deep cleft between bold hill
features, then rising to overlook magnificent prospects with
the snow-capped Miella gleaming brightly in the north.
Depressing damage had been wrought along the right-of-way
of the lateral railway which runs between Benevento and
Termoli.

Vasto was the ancient Istonium. What fascination that
fact may have had for us was utterly dissipated by mud and
ruins. We followed the TAC. 35 signs and soon located
"Ops." and the Canadian Liaison Officer, Major "Dick"
Malone. Following lunch we moved on a strange, little box-
like building with crenellated towers and Moslem windows and
Dick showed us a small room in which he thought we might
hang the paintings. The walls were covered with a preposterous "Recketts Blue" checkerboard wallpaper. We placed
one sketch near and screamed "No" in unison. A platoon of
men moved the heavy furniture out of a hall and in an hour
we had the fifty-four paintings hanging there, a bit crowded
possibly, but there they were in Vasto.

The dashing 12th Hussar aide, Captain "Johnny" Hender-
son had suggested that the General could be expected at about
half past four. Ogilvie and I had scarcely time to consider
what we might do until that hour, when General Bernard
Montgomery (now Field-Marshal Lord Montgomery of
Alamein) suddenly appeared in the doorway. Over battledress he wore a sheepskin-lined leather jacket and his famous
black beret, with its two badges. Not ten minutes had elapsed
since we had finished hanging the last picture. We could not
credit this sudden appearance to his impatience to see the
show, after all, at that time he was planning the Sangro operation, but he was employing the tactical principle of surprise
with considerable success.

He approached with a cheerful smile, shook hands and
then, adjusting tortoise-shell glasses, began a most careful
study of each work. He complimented us on our enterprise at
Campobasso, and drew Ogilvie into a discussion concerning his

American L.C.I. Transporting Canadian Troops from Philippeville, Algeria, to Taranto, Italy. Mount Etna, Sicily, in background.

"Stand Easy" Following Crash Action. Northwest of Campobasso, Italy.

drawing of Canadian Engineers, erecting a Bailey bridge under fire. We were impressed by his interested comment and cordial manner. He looked at the paintings with a soldier's eye for detail and fitness; they reminded him of incidents and places. After spending far more time than we thought a General officer might be expected to spend, he turned and thanked us both, in a most charming way, and invited us to tea in his mess at 1630 hours.

The tea was rather formal, and a bit austere by "E" mess standards, but for us a new and interesting experience. The Army Commander sat at the top of a large T-shaped table arrangement, flanked by Brigadier Graham on his left, his Chief of Staff, Major General Riley, on his right, with other impressive officers supporting them. Ogilvie and I sat with the junior officers, on either side of the descender of the "T", profoundly impressed by this great array of military talent. There were moments of light, witty conversation, but no smoking. We were a bit startled and surprised when, with a rather loud scraping of chairs, the whole function ended abruptly as the General rose from his seat and left with his aides and immediate staff.

*   *   *

When we returned to Main 40, Divisional Headquarters had moved from its location beside the drove road to billets in Campobasso. "E" mess, to which Ogilvie, Hughes and I belonged, along with eleven others, was assigned space in a second-floor flat on the Via Cavour.

It was a fantastic place, a theatrical confusion of pompous, late nineteenth century, middle-class grandeur, incredible wallpapers, tasseled velour drapes, and portieres in puce and taupe. A canopied, rococo, double bed stood in one of the three bedrooms. Provocative, life-size nude putti, carved in high relief, frolicked across the head and footboards, evoking hilarious nonsense from Mickey Burch and Kim Arnold, who slept in it. The billeting officers having permitted the tenants to remove their bedding and such other possessions as they wished, we simply placed our separate bedrolls on the empty bedsprings or, in some cases, on the floor. The apartment was without heat or water. Army generators provided only sporadic and limited periods of light. But we were all grateful to be under a roof and temporarily out of the rain.

Headquarters was agog with the latest move. Third Brigade had gone off alone, on a diversionary operation into the mountains. The story was that the high command wanted the operation to be as pretentious as possible, in fact it was to appear as if the whole division were committed. Yet, when Ogilvie and I signified our intention of following, we were discouraged in the firmest terms, and told that non-operational vehicles would not be permitted on the road.

Torrential rains were falling, accompanied by thunder and lightning. Deserted, immobilized, miserable and depressed, Ogilvie and I decided to go to the Aldershot Club to seek consolation and whomever we might find there. Sure enough, there were the despised and the rejected, war correspondents, public relations officers, reinforcements and replacements, all moping over bottles of vino roso. It was there that we met Art Holmes, Lloyd Moore and Bob Campbell, who had arrived in Italy recently with the convoy which had brought the 5th Canadian Armoured Division. They seemed to consider themselves lucky to be alive. Three vessels had been sunk and, apart from the heavy loss of life, the complete equipment for No. 14 Canadian General Hospital had been lost, together with supplies and equipment for the Canadian Dental Corps, and all the mail.

This depressing story did not improve our mental health and we returned to our billets in silence. It continued cold and unseasonably wet. The tedium of these dog days was appalling.

*   *   *

Yesterday we had gone to Divisional Headquarters in the *Scuola Elementare*. Since it was impossible to work outdoors, or in our crowded billet, we had decided to request a room in

the school, where both the historians and artists might carry
on projects in hand. We found that the Camp Commandant
was off with the Brigade, and no one had the authority to
assign accommodation.

We returned this morning and Major Richardson very
reluctantly assigned a room to us. Quite empty, it contained
neither table nor chair, had no lock on the door (a primary
requisite at a Divisional Headquarters), and several panes of
glass were missing from the windows, making the place as cold
and draughty as King and Yonge on a January morning. But
it was space and we were grateful for it. While we were
considering how we might remedy its many shortcomings, a
Signals Officer appeared at the door and announced that it was
his space and that R.H.Q. Sigs. was to be set up there immediately. We bowed deeply and surrendered, secretly hoping that
we might find a more agreeable room.

*   *   *

"E" mess is approached under an archway leading off the
Via Cavour. The archway leads to a courtyard where a
garden may once have existed. Tonight a pig tethered by one
of its hind legs emits melancholy squeals as if anticipating its
eventual fate. A stone-stepped staircase leads to the mess on
the second floor. We are attempting to reduce the damp chill
of the place with the assistance of an open charcoal brazier.
Due to the diversionary operation, the personnel of "E" mess
is reduced to eight. The table is set for supper, fancy china
over a lace cloth, a little exotic perhaps, but then while it lasts,
why not? Doc Byers and Bob Wilson are fussing around the
radio which Frank Nutall has somehow and somewhere had
put in working order. One of the nightly events at Campobasso which has fascinated us all is the languorous sexy singing
of "Lili Marlene" preceding the German news in English from
radio Belgrade. It is a must for everyone who can get near
the Signals truck or a radio. The news which follows is either
promptly turned off or listened to mid rounds of derisive

laughter, particularly those bulletins which deal with the success of the German forces in Italy.

"Wie einst Lili Marlene, wie einst Lili Marlene." Tenderly, and with haunting effectiveness Lale Anderson broods over this love song and many a lonely soldier is swept away on the currents of emotion which well up in his lonely heart, as this devastating war song reflects the frustrations of his own love-life.

> Vor de Kaserne, vor dem grossen tor
> Stand eine laterne un steht sie noch davor.
> So wall'n wir uns da wiederseh'n
> Bei der laterne woll'n wir steh'n
> Wie einst Lili Marlene, wie einst Lili Marlene.

Everyone hums or whistles the melody. Our German interrogators sing it in German, Isolani sings it in Italian, most of us have one or other of the many English translations, some with the beauty of poetry, others perversely obscene, all finding consolation in an extraordinary enemy love song which has become the favourite of two opposing armies. . . .

*   *   *

It had rained heavily all night and a misty drizzle fell as we walked over to the *Scuola Elementare*. Major Richardson could not be found but a Sergeant in the Camp office said the room was ours, and that Sigs. had found something more comfortable. We winced as we thanked him and made our way down to the empty space; there it was, the floor wet from the rain that had blown in during the night. We pulled ourselves together and began a recce of the school in the hope of salvaging some furnishings.

Inside the first unlocked door we found a table which was surreptitiously spirited away, then followed a school form and a chair and a quantity of cardboard. Thus equipped, we opened our war art botega in Campobasso. Our most urgent and essential need was now a hasp and padlock for we knew only too well that if we left the room unguarded for a moment, all would be lost. This problem was fortunately solved for us by our new driver, Nicholls, who found these requirements in the visitors' car park.

The drizzle ceased. Although there were no signs of clearing we were impatient to get some painting done outdoors. The 15 cwt. had been returned from the workshop that morning. The new driver Nicholls is a straightforward honest farm boy from Bolton, touched that we know his hometown district, responding well to our glowing memories of the hills around Palgrave and the idiosyncracies of Miss Matson, owner of the Queen's Hotel there.

We drove north through Oratino toward the Biferno diversion. Approaching the crossing the road was jammed with R.E. vehicles. Will and I walked forward to the river and appreciated the problem. It was a wild tossing torrent in full flood spate about eighty yards wide and the colour of bean soup. Obviously no one was going to get across for some time. We went back on the road a mile or so to a blown bridge over a deep gully. The abutments were still standing and on one of these we harboured the vehicle and recced for a painting location. The demolition charge which had blown the bridge must have been very heavy indeed, for the masonry which had constituted two arches was scattered over a wide radius, and the steel central span lay twisted and rusting eighty feet below in the gully. The diversion our forces had created lay in a deep loop to the east of the wreckage, otherwise the scene around us was one of classic nobility. We flattered ourselves by suggesting that it had some kinship to the landscapes of Claude Lorraine or Richard Wilson. In front of us was a high pinnacle of rock, on which the magnificent ruin of an ancient watch tower stood. Behind that the snow-covered peaks of the Matese were hidden in blustery cloud. To the left stood the picturesque hilltown of Roccaspromonte. Only now, well past the middle of November, were signs of autumn colour noticeable in the lush forestry that clothed the hills. We settled to our work and immediately became conscious of the marrow-chilling cold.

About mid-afternoon, while we were making good progress, a villainous cloud crept over the Matese and headed toward us. We worked until the first incredibly large drops of rain fell and then bundled everything into the back of the truck. The cloudburst that broke over us continued with such violence that we thought it must end as suddenly as it had begun, but after an hour or so it still continued and the failing light showed the day to be over. On the way back to town we were sorely tempted to pick up the refugees who trudged beside the road, drenched to the skin, but a standing order forbade our carrying civilians at any time or under any circumstances.

"E" mess looked and felt comfortable that evening. The brazier was doing a good job in the combined living- and dining-room. The bedroom, however, which I shared with Ogilvie, Doc Byers and Bill Deery, was still as cold as the grave. Douglas LaChance was in from the Brigade front, now reaching into the headwaters hilltown of Castel di Sangro. He chilled us with stories of the enemy approach to preparing a winter line. They had cleared a wide area of all inhabitants, and then systematically demolished every house, barn and shed, in order to reduce attacking cover and provide clear fields of fire for the defenders. Farmers and townsmen had been carefully screened. Every able-bodied male had been sent to the Todt organization; all animals, fowl and stored crops had been requisitioned; the aged, the women and the children had been driven toward our lines to become a heavy charge on the limited facilities we had for their care and feeding. He reported that the Brigade was doing well under most exasperating physical conditions.

*   *   *

Ogilvie had been delighted to receive a signal from Lt.-Col. W. F. K. Thompson, C.O. of the 1st Air Light Landing Regt., 1st British Airborne Division. The message complimented him on a painting he had exhibited in our Campobasso exhibition in which he had depicted Colonel Thompson's unit in an action somewhere further south. The message also extended a very cordial invitation to both Ogilvie and me to come over and do further work with his men in their present location, and since the A.L.L. Regt. was attached to our Division, it was quite within the terms of our directive to accept. So two days later, on a grey uncertain morning we packed the 15 cwt. for the journey. This meant painting equipment, bedrolls and rations for three men for three days. Mid-morning the sky cleared and to our great pleasure a glorious Indian-summer day beamed down on us.

The route was an impressive one. First through the town of Vinchiature and then through the sunshine to Boiano at the very foot of the snow-capped massif. We then turned on to a rough secondary road through Monteverdi and Spinetti. At mid-day we stopped by the roadside, boiled up some tea and had our lunch.

Santa Elena was a small town high up in the Matese, a tightly-packed concentration of habitations, flanking a narrow cobbled thoroughfare, picturesque, but hygienically primitive. We experienced no difficulty in finding the Air Light Landing command post where the adjutant, Captain Hanhart, received us and directed us to a second-floor billet above a bakery on the Via Mazzini. It was empty but clean and smelled faintly of freshly baked bread. After carrying our bedrolls and equipment up to our new digs, we just had time to return to the H.Q. mess for tea. There we met Colonel Thompson, the famous *"alto colonello."* He was, as the legend described him, an immensely tall young man, with great personal charm and lots of aggressive go. Both he and his 2 i/c, Major Jones, immediately outlined the plan of work they had arranged for us. It sounded formidable, but we kept that point of view to ourselves and listened with attentive interest.

The 1st Air Light Landing Regiment was an extremely mobile and hard-hitting artillery force, armed with the 75 mm. American pack howitzer. These astounding weapons are normally towed by jeeps, all of which could be landed by glider,

In the present situation, where their role was clearing the enemy from remote mountain locations, they had adopted mules as their motive power and had proved extremely effective in their work with our Division.

At nineteen thirty hours we assembled again for dinner. The dinner and conversation which followed was as select as the brandy and it was with some difficulty that Ogilvie and I found our billet in the primeval darkness that existed in the street when we left the mess.

*   *   *

It poured rain most of the night and the morning was dark and infinitely depressing, but the indefatigable Thompson was as cheery as a meadowlark and had everything teed-up on schedule, racing about on what appeared to be a kiddy's bike with wheels twelve inches in diameter. He led off with the gun itself which was assembled before our eyes with tournament skill and dexterity. We had elected to make pencil sketches, but I had scarcely put two lines to paper when another downpour swept on us from the hills, drenching us before we were driven to cover. All morning we pursued the Colonel's programme hopelessly behind schedule, alternating between fifteen minutes clear and forty of rain, until the whole experience became an ordeal. We did deal with the gun and the limber and the mine clearance, and the men, who were magnificent specimens, the ideal prototype of the paratrooper, but it was a struggle and we were relieved when Capt. Harrison took us to one of the Battery messes for lunch.

This meal was brightened by the presence of two padres from 13th Corp, Capt. Dow (R.C.) and Capt. Gray (C. of E.). While we discussed the Madonna and Child for the Northampton Cathedral, by Henry Moore, and the possibility of a post-war revival in the liturgical arts, the rain changed to hail and it became much colder. During the afternoon the same problem of shower-dodging plagued us, but we

had now become determined; we just could not give up with
these English gunners watching our every move.   We were
wet through and mud to the knees as we worked on the
emplaced gun; if our sketches reflect these conditions it is not
surprising.   As darkness fell we returned to our billet, wet
and discouraged.   Outside a fresh torrent poured from an
unfriendly sky.

*   *   *

Morning was as black as a boot-heel.   I had been awakened
at O-five-twenty hours by the 1st Air Light Landing Regiment
pulling out of town.   With this unexpected and unexplained
departure had gone our opportunity of drawing the Sherman
pack employed by Colonel Thompson when elements of his
regiment forded the Biferno in close pursuit of the enemy.
On that occasion they had dismantled their guns and packed
them on the top of Sherman tanks of the Canadian Armoured
Brigade.   The Colonel was a legend in Campobasso.   He had
fought his guns as close support weapons in the advance on
that town and beyond, fording the Biferno to Castropignano
and Torella del Sannio.   During the fighting immediately north
of Campobasso, he had climbed to the topmost keep of the
Castello under heavy enemy fire and "fooed" his own guns
from that magnificent observation post.   The padre from the
nearby church of Santa Maria Maggiore proudly told us the
story of the brave *Alto Colonello* who had dared enemy fire
to chase the Tedeschi from the district.
   We left Santa Elena and drove to the crossroads of
Masseria Piano and there pulled off the road, lit a fire, and
cooked our breakfast.   It was a cold dark impressive
morning with mountainous cumulus breaking over the indigo
hills, permitting occasional flashes of early sunshine.   Autumn
colouring could now be said to be at its height.   It did not
achieve the brilliant hues we know so well in eastern Canada,
it was much more sober.   A rich russet pervaded the scene,
contrasting agreeably with the dark blue of the mountains to

make a striking setting for the early morning sky. Tea and
fat bacon made a satisfying breakfast.

*   *   *

Like most Italian towns, Campobasso can look back at
a very long history, alternating between despotism and violence
on the one hand, and sublime periods of vegetable existence on
the other. Unlike the glamorous centres of culture and
administration, in the west and north of Italy, its long story
has not attracted fashionable writers or travellers. The fact
that nothing, even of a documentary character, had been found
concerning the history of the town during our stay, made it an
excellent subject for discussion by the creative brains of "E"
mess.

The town is not an obvious place. Even the experienced
traveller in peacetime might be excused if he passed it by.
There are no great monuments of art there, no art
galleries. The cathedral, dedicated to the Holy Trinity, *Santa
Trinata,* is an early 19th century neo-classic revival with a
very severe Ionic portico and a droll interior. Yet Campobasso has an undeniable fascination for the patient observer
who is perceptive and willing to search. In the middle of a twentieth century world war, we were of course seeing it at its
worst, bereft of its young men, denied any civic prerogatives,
shelled first by ourselves and then by the enemy, and now
drenched by cold winter rains. Yet in spite of these overwhelming disadvantages the town maintained an impressive
dignity of its own. The newer part, the *Borgo Nuovo,* was
generously laid out in an expansive civic style, characteristic of
the upsurge of national consciousness which followed unity in
1870. The street plan was delightfully irregular, but with
some straight, well-turfed and planted boulevards. Tumultuous modern baroque appeared through trimmed ilex, and
austere new fascist structures and modern apartment blocks
were flanked by cypress and fronted by gardens.

In contrast, the old town, the *Borgo San Antonio,* huddled picturesquely about the base of the castle rock, its narrow cobbled viccoli climbing the steep south-east slope which rises to the piazzale fronting the castle, three hundred feet above. The old town was unique and apart from the modern city, a surviving remnant of an almost forgotten past, with its vestiges of an early wall and its dependence on the grim old castle above. Conversely, the castle owed a debt to these clustering swallow-nest habitations and the vassals and villeins who served and fought for their lord protector. Today the donkey paths which lead up to the castle from the old town are seldom used, and a new carefully graded road swept widely around the rock, looping up its eastern flank between rows of impressive stone pines. The old economic, administrative and military ties between castle and town are gone with the lords and serfs, and today the rugged old building is just a picturesque curiosity.

*   *   *

The sun shone brightly for the first time in weeks. It was Friday the 26th and Ogilvie and I hurried over to the *Scuola,* filled with renewed energies as the sun streamed down on us from a clear sky. For days "E" mess had vibrated with rumour, adding up to the possibility of movement. Some had it that we were bound for the Adriatic coast where we would embark for Jugoslavia or Albania; others that it would be either Bari, Taranto, or Potenza where, together with the 5th Canadian Armoured Div., we would form a Canadian Corps destined for a fresh seaborne invasion.

Back in our schoolroom studio, we had just settled to work when Charles Richardson appeared and told us we would have to vacate immediately. Third Brigade was to remain under 13th Corps in action, but tactical H.Q. were returning and must be accommodated. He had assigned our room to the C.R.E. We thanked him for letting us know and, as if with the burden of long suffering humanity on our shoulders, we began to pack our equipment. While we were engaged in this familiar procedure, Sergeant Taylor, the section's clerk, appeared to say that a "most immediate" signal had been circulated, warning that Division H.Q. was to stand ready to move out of Campobasso on the 29th. This announcement cleared the air a bit and we completed our pack and lugged everything back to the mess on Via Cavour.

*   *   *

Campobasso is by no means the most beautiful town in Italy. In fact, standing in the Piazza Gabrielle Peppe in the new section, it is difficult to appreciate that it is located high in the eastern slopes of the Appenines. However, on our last day in town and in billets, Ogilvie and I made a grand tour of those quiet places which had interested us. The weather we had had and our physical experience had been misery itself, and yet for some unexplained reason we had formed an attachment for the place. Santa Trinata, a dark cold church, always peopled with coughing worshippers, the Municipio, where we had first gone with Cottam six weeks ago, and then the castle itself. The ruin we now surveyed was built by Nicollo Monforte at about the time of Cartier's voyages. It was, of course constructed over the remains of an earlier stronghold which showed unmistakable signs of the Hohenstaufen builders, and no doubt the impregnable character of the site would have appealed to the feudal lords of even earlier days. The top brains in "E" mess liked to believe in the possibility that Nicollo Monforte was a descendant of Simon de Montfort, the great English statesman of Henry III's reign. It is a fact that Simon's third son, Guy, came to Italy for the homicidal purpose of revenging his father's death. After accomplishing this grim mission, by murdering Henry's son, the Duke of Cornwall, while he knelt at worship in San Silvestro at Viterbo, he joined the forces of Charles of Anjou. We know that Charles admired Guy's spirit and his abilities as a soldier and rewarded him with high military honours in the Kingdom of the two Sicilies. Since

Guy married and settled in that Kingdom, which includes Campobasso, it seems not an unreasonable conjecture that in time the name of his descendants may have taken on the Italian form Monforte. This, I believe, was Hughes' conclusion. Of course the arguments for and against this possibility were almost equally divided, and even if the contention is unsupported by any real evidence, it proved to be one of the liveliest and most engaging fictions created in "E" mess.

The mess echoed with noisy jubilation as spirits soared in that wild excitement that precedes movement. The Division was not longer "At Rest"; we were on our way. Leaving the high terraces, the battlements, the keeps and the platforms. The Campobasso story was ending, at least for a time. Everyone was examining and checking equipment with the utmost care, because the Division was committed to a winter fight, and there was no question about the fact that it would be grim. We were leaving the ashen skies, the cold numbing rains, leaving it all and starting afresh, a new location, new problems and fears, perhaps. But we were on our way and who cared. "Wie einst Lili Marlene, wie einst Lili Marlene. . . ."

PART

III

ORTONA

It was still quite dark when Bill Deery roused us at 0445 hours on that last morning in Campobasso. The movement order had been circulated and we knew officially the route we would follow that day to reach the first staging camp, designated as Petacciato. The approach march to the battle-line was to take possibly three days, then once committed we would strike hard and fast toward Pescara.

We were on the move again, racing toward the grimmest action of the campaign. Happily we were innocent of that fact, and spirits ran high as we sighted the blue waters of the Adriatic from above Casacalenda, and far out on the horizon the Tremitii islands, shimmering in the sunshine.

Bombers and fighters shuttled north on missions deep into enemy territory and south again for another lethal load. We presented a most vulnerable target in the warm autumn sunshine and were glad that the Luftwaffe were conspicuous by their absence.

We crossed the Biferno and wound through Termoli, past the "Three Rivers" battleground, saluting the rusting hulk of

"Barbaric" as we passed. All about us, yokes of white oxen ploughed the bloody groves, heedless of the living or the dead. To our surprise, Petacciato fell behind and we crossed the Trigno. On the reverse slope, leading to San Salvo, "Camp" directed us into a muddy olive grove. Stage one had been completed.

*   *   *

December had come, a violent, desperate month of bitter fighting in a macabre setting. The drama was intense, a bleak stage stripped of all but the most brutal properties, swept by gales and rain, under a flying wrack of dark cloud; a sinister stage, filled with terror and tumult, where courage and hope marched with despair and misery; a bloody stage, where grim determination hacked and slashed away with fanatical resistance to the grisly end. We were hurrying forward to overwhelm an enemy who had been forced to abandon his chosen winter line, had been turfed out of his deep Shelters along the Sangro and who, at this moment, was running for the next promising bit of cover. There might be a rear-guard action, but he would not stop, he could not, if we pressed him hard enough. Pescara; it did not look far on the map, forty-five miles at the most. A week, maybe ten days, should see us there, and then the pincer move through the mountains to Rome. We were filled with headlong optimism as we camouflaged the vehicles and raised our tarpaulin shelter at San Salvo. Even as we made camp the rains began which were to plague us, and to turn this and all other olive groves into intractable mud-holes.

Next morning we learned that only one Bailey had withstood the fury of a flash-flood on the Sangro, and that a serious traffic bottleneck had resulted. Our turn to cross the river would not come until at least the following day.

There was great satisfaction in the knowledge that Second Canadian Infantry Brigade was already across the Sangro river and moving forward to the support of the British division then in contact. Ken Cottam was full of enthusiasm; he had been detailed to see the New Zealand divisional intelligence somewhere near Atessa on that rainy morning. Would Ogilvie and I like to go along? We knew that the New Zealanders had with them Peter McIntyre as war artist, and we appreciated this opportunity of contacting him. Cottam expected that we would be back long before dark that day and, since there was no chance of movement, Hughes gave us his blessing.

Atessa was some twenty-five miles to the west of San Salvo and on our side of the Sangro, so off we went in the "I" jeep. Beyond Cupello we left the coastal plain and began twisting and turning over switch-back hills. As usual, diversions were plentiful. But we had left the charred path of battle and we became intrigued with the wild beauty that spread all about us. Beyond Gissi we were in Laurentian country, above which the snow-capped beacon of Monte Amaro gleamed with an incandescent light. As we approached the mountains it became increasingly cold, compared with the mild coastal climate we had left behind.

Then the unexpected happened. As we descended into a valley we encountered two three-ton trucks, one of which was stuck axle-deep in the diversion ford across a small stream. Vigorous profanity echoed in the pastoral silence, as the drivers struggled with the problem. For us, it began as a welcome halt, but after an hour had passed, we knew that if the diversion were not cleared soon we should not reach our destination before dark. We also realized that a return to the Division that day was even then out of the question. Finally a winch, supplemented by a tow-line, did the trick and we entered Atessa as darkness fell.

Atessa was a gaunt, hollow-eyed little hill-town, with a sweeping view of the Maiella on the one hand, and the Adriatic on the other. Except for demolitions it had escaped serious war damage and there had been no shelling. It swarmed with people, largely refugees. Even its normal population of ten thousand must have taxed its capacity. One wondered where this wartime overflow found shelter.

We had no alternative but to remain overnight and we realized that accommodation in so crowded a community would be a problem. But at the Amgot office we were received with surprising goodwill by two cheerful young American officers, Lieut. Stauffler from New York, a Vice-President of Abercrombie & Fitch, who looked a little out of character in Atessa, and his colleague, a school teacher from Danbury, Connecticut. When they learned the circumstances of our visit, nothing seemed too much trouble to meet our needs. The Podesta was called into a prolonged conference on accommodation, following which we were led out into the darkness, borne down by five blankets each and several cans of food.

To our interested surprise, our guide led us to the Bishop's Palace, where we were shown rooms before being presented to His Grace, the Bishop of Triventi, and to his brother, a refugee from another community, and to the brother's numerous and charming family. The Bishop, in long black soutane and silk cap, was most cordial, an attitude which lost none of its genuineness when he discovered that we were all Protestants.

He led us into the dining-room and seated us at a table covered with a white cloth, lit by candles, and centred by a bowl of oranges. After a prolonged prayer, we conversed in awkward English and Italian, keeping tactfully off the subject of our mission. His questions were about Canada: Where did Ogilvie and I come from? What was the country like? When I told him it was near the Huron country, where the Jesuit missions had been in the 17th century, he became quite excited, and I found he knew a great deal about that tragic story. We were served pasta, followed by meat with bread and the red wine of the district. Vinia, a niece, hovered about, a petite child of about eight, wearing pigtails. Carlo, one of the nephews, possibly fifteen, was studying English and most anxious to converse with us.

I had an excellent night's rest in a large room, overlooking a conglomeration of tiled roofs, toward the high peaks of the Miella. Above my bed was an enormous crucifix, three feet high. Hanging from it was a bleeding Christ, a tortured figure that seemed to symbolize the agony which humanity was suffering at that very moment.

By morning our concern was that the Division might already have moved and that we had better rejoin them without further loss of time. Cottam had contacted the New Zealand division. Much to our regret we had been unable to locate Captain McIntyre. We offered our thanks and said our adieus to the Bishop.

It was a crisp shining morning, after yesterday's rain, and the vast trench which is the valley of the Sangro spread out majestically on our left as we edged carefully over the unswept road to Paglieta. Firing was continuous and great columns of black smoke rose from undisclosed sources along the northern slope of the valley which had been the intended German winter line. The air too was filled with action, aircraft miraculously passing through tight group of ack-ack as if impervious to the flak that must have screamed about them. The scene was stupendous: behind us Monte Amaro rose in lofty silence, the course of the great river curving serenely on the floor of its mile-wide valley, the Adriatic refracting the blinding morning sunshine as we rode our sky-line trail.

Leaving Paglieta, we could see the masonry bridge that carried the highway across the Sangro. It was a masterly job of demolition, every arch blown. We could also see a Bailey just east of it, black with north-bound traffic. The cannonading was continuous and an umbrella of fighters roared above the crossing, while above them again, flights of Mitchels and Kittyhawks moved north and south in endless procession. We were back in the battle.

We turned south through Torino, a village with a narrow one-way track of a street that rose in a steep gradient between lofty balconied habitations. These village defiles must be a worry to the command. They are romantically beautiful, but a headache for military traffic where time is a factor. We started meeting Main 40 vehicles just north of Casalbordino. This was a stroke of luck we had hardly expected. The movement north had resumed early that morning. We turned into the barely moving column, heading once more for the Sangro crossing.

*   *   *

The day proved long and tiring and it was late afternoon when we awaited our turn to descend a freshly bull-dozed trail to the second and most easterly of the Bailey bridges. In spite of our air umbrella, the Luftwaffe made noisy but ineffectual efforts to bomb the column. They appeared to be more successful on the north side of the river and from our screen of trees we could see the bombs, like hotwater heaters, dropping to their targets. The air was filled with the pressures of concussion and the spectacular ack-ack barrage decorated the sky with deadly plumage.

As the sun set we started to move cautiously down the improvised trail to the bridge. Less fortunate vehicles lay upturned in the bracken to the right and left. When a vehicle became mired or bogged, or broke an axle, it was rolled off the trail and recovered later, rather than allow it to hold up the column. Needless to say, the drivers exercised extraordinary care in making the descent. We emerged onto the floor of the valley in good order and followed a taped trail to the Bailey as seven successive bomb bursts raked the north shore. The towering smoke columns darkened the sunset sky, obscuring the blue silhouette of the Maiella in the background.

*   *   *

Main 40 spent two nights on the north side of the Sangro beside the railway station at Fossacesia. We broke camp at first light on the second morning and packed for the move. We were across the river obstacle and the heat was on again.

The convoy climbed the hill from sea level to that of the coastal plain, preceded by bulldozers who cleared an ineffectual road-block of *live* olive trees. Acre after acre of productive olives had been hacked down and strewn along the road to impede progress or to divert us to a mined road at a lower level. We were shocked and depressed by this wanton destruction, for the only purpose it accomplished was the ruin of some hard-working peasant grower and it did nothing to obstruct our movement. The town of Fossacesia, perched vulnerably on the Sangro ridge, was a roofless jagged ruin. The church of San Donat, showing marked indications of a Gothic origin, had three charred walls emerging from the rubble. On these, the subtle colour of ageing frescoes brooded tenderly over a setting of utter ruin.

The plain beyond the town was dismal in the extreme. Mile after monotonous mile of olive groves, depressingly grey and alike in the drizzle. Troops of the Hastings and Prince Edward Regiment marched in single file at the side of the road, gas capes glistening in the rain. Occasionally they shouted some profane jibe at the passing truck drivers and an equally unsavory retort followed. Mid-morning the Camp Commandant appeared beside the road and directed us into another anonymous olive grove, recently ploughed. We harboured the vehicles, stretched the camouflage nets and started to dig our slit trenches.

*   *   *

We had spent a sleepless and terrifying night. Seventeen centimetre shells screamed over our heads in bewildering sequence. Hardly had the deafening echo of one hellish crash subsided when two, three-four-five followed in quick succession. The three of us lay quaking in a shallow slit trench. It was not a visual experience but a tense, exhausting, bowel-gripping nightmare. We knelt with our heads bent as low as we could get them, pressing into the wet earth, wondering if this might not be our last night? Every lull that lasted more than thirty seconds we spent in deepening and improving our cover. To the right and left we could see spoil being tossed by other anxious diggers, until the next pattern of shells screamed into the valley, when we would all immediately scuttle into the earth with the speed of frightened beetles.

Violent shattering sound filled the night. When the Jerry gunners rested, if ever they did, our own boys took over with counter-battery fire that equalled the enemy effort in intensity.

We felt as grey as the dawn when it came, and we looked it. But with the growing light we laughed at it all. Someone yelled, "You guys still alive?" "Barely" was the response. The shelling had finally subsided into normal desultory fire at about 0430 hours. Since it had begun at dusk we had had nearly twelve hours of continuous shell fire.

*   *   *

Ogilvie and I had moved forward from Main 40 to 2nd Brigade H.Q. on the previous day. The Brigade Major, Major "Bill" Woods, did not seem too happy to see us, an attitude we both understood. He was a busy man and had no desire to add to his burden by cluttering the Headquarters with non-operational vehicles. On our part, we were anxious to see as much of the action as might be permitted. If we were to paint this battle, we had to appreciate something of its character.

Staff Captain Conway directed us to the ploughed field where we had just spent the night. There we lost no time in harbouring and concealing the Humber and needed no encouragement to start digging. Earlier that morning we had learned that our own Mess President, Captain "Bill" Hall, M.C., of Ottawa, had been severely wounded and might lose his right foot. Later, I was leaving the mess tent with Doc. Byers when, out of the sun, came the sudden roar of aircraft, machine guns blazing. I just recall registering the appearance of four M.E. 109's with four Spitfires in hot pursuit, the sun glinting on the bombs as they started their curving descent. The Doc and I hit the dirt and stayed there until it was all over. As I say, we needed no encouragement to start digging. Before the serious shelling began at dusk, we had a trench where fair kneeling cover could be had.

I unpacked my equipment and started a painting which
included the skyline of San Vito. Second Brigade Headquarters was astride the San Apollinaire road, on the reverse
slope of the Feltrino River valley, immediately north of San
Vito Chietino. The location was believed to be dead ground,
as far as shelling was concerned. Tragically enough this was
soon proved to be quite wrong. Like so many of these coastal
towns, San Vito is built on a promontory, formed by the
south bank of the river, with an expansive belvedere facing
the sea. Enemy shelling was continuing and several fires
raged unchecked along the dark skyline.

I had barely finished the drawing when a drizzle of rain
set in and, since I was working with water-colours, before
very long I was rained out. Ogilvie had a similar experience
sketching the prisoners Cottam was interrogating. Our
ploughed field was soon converted into a sienna-coloured
quagmire as the rain blew in sheets from the sea. We
struggled ineffectually with drainage around the bivy, but
we were helpless to do anything about the slit-trench and
inches of water had already collected in the bottom. Then
someone suggested a sump and a duckboard raised on bricks.
Cottam thought this was practical and suggested a trip in
his jeep to Marino di San Vito, where we could easily salvage
the materials, as well as possibly finding some oranges or
nuts for sale.

Marino skirted the base of the promontory on which
the town stood. The railway station was there and a small
harbour for fishing boats, empty on this dismal day. South
of Marino a picturesque coastal road extended and gave
access to several empty but attractive villas with overgrown
and neglected gardens. We were told that in one of these
Gabriele d'Annunzio had written his famous novel, *The
Triumph of Death*. This may well have been true, though
our informant was discreetly vague about the precise location
of the villa and cleverly evaded our further inquiry by directing us to a nearby orange grove. Fresh fruit held a far
greater appeal that afternoon and we soon found ourselves

in a fantastic garden. Flowering loquat, olives, figs, grapes,
white asters, golden and pink chrysanthemums and, above
all, oranges. The trees, shining in the rain, glowed with
bright golden fruit. They looked unreal, artificial, yet there
they were. It seemed incredible that so much natural beauty
should exist beside so much deadly scrofulous discomfort.
As we moved to enter this paradise Cottam warned, "Watch
for mines! Let me go first!" We were still on earth, still
at war, danger lurked all about us, even in this sublime garden.
We pulled the fruit and sucked at it greedily. Fresh ripe fruit
was an extraordinary treat; the cool juice dripped from our
chins and ran up our sleeves. It was a long time since we
had had anything fresh; we seemed starved for what those
oranges contained. Then one of us gagged, I think it was
Cottam. He had come across an inch-square shell fragment
at the centre of one fruit. Even this grove then had not
escaped. Yet it seemed so remote and disarmingly secure.

Above us in the town, the shelling was desultory. The
daylight lull was still on, but there was no cessation of activity.
We returned through Marino, picking up from among the
ruins of several buildings the material to floor our slit-trench.

*   *   *

Back at the Brigade, we felt refreshed after our outing
and better prepared to meet the tensions that were becoming
so familiar. At "Ops" we tried to piece together a picture
of the struggle proceeding in the Moro valley, a mile north
of the Headquarters. On the next bench of the adjoining
vineyard, a battery of three-inch mortars were taking on
a target in handbook style. A three-inch mortar is a jolting
distraction at any time and our efforts to appreciate the
battle were punctuated by the precision work of well-trained
crews. We learned that the P.P.C.L.I. and elements of
the 44th Royal Tank Regiment were being heavily counter-
attacked. They had established a shaky bridgehead across
the Moro at or near Roatti. The tanks had of necessity

forded the stream and then daringly climbed the narrow winding road that hair-pinned up the northern slope of the valley to the village. The rain was adding to supply difficulties and making withdrawal well nigh impossible, even if it seemed expedient.

Darkness came at 1630 hours. Our mediums had been firing a terrific barrage since mid-afternoon with the enemy responding in kind, paying close attention to the supply road and the Bailey bridge below our bivy. At 1800 hours an ominous silence fell on the area. He might just be having more bread and sausage, but we were uneasy.

The almost unbearable silence lasted for two hours, but at a few minutes past eight he opened up. Ogilvie and I had just turned in, may have had possibly forty winks, when the first shell seared the top of our bivy. We were fully clothed, of course, but on went the rubber boots, the trench coats, and the tin hats, and we were in the slit-trench before we were fully awake. That was the last sleep we had until morning. The first long barrage lasted from 2003 hours until 0007 when there was a brief lull. We did crawl back to the bivy once or twice, but a particularly close burst, or the terrifying sound of fragmentation slashing through foliage and shrubbery, drove us back below ground time and time again. A lull seemed to come about midnight but it was short-lived and barely gave us time to stretch our paralyzed limbs. We did relax a moment on our blankets, but I was just enjoying a good yawning stretch when down came the barrage again, *allegro vivace*. For a moment or two we continued to lie still, listening tensely to the falsetto shriek of the shells as they dropped to their target. In this narrow valley, the burst of a seventeen centimetre shell is like the soul-shaking crack of doom. If you are tired, as undoubtedly we were, it jars the brain with unmerciful violence and then reverberates and echoes in the darkness in grotesque and terrifying spirals of dissonance. It is difficult, if not impossible, to convey any impression of the frightening strain of continuous exposure to shell-fire. Life seems temporarily suspended. In a trance-like state of uncertainty and fear, the weird imagery of the supernatural alternates with the painful consciousness of physical danger. The pounding heart beats like timpani in the breast, nerves are taut and vibrate with demonic music. The throbbing bloodstream pounds a brutal tattoo within one's nakedness. Reality and unreality intermingle in the mutilating darkness. Wild hallucinations burst in the mind with a flash of piercing light, revealing the chalky shadows of a vague past and the surging reality of the present. The fear of death does not seem to have the same urgency as a mute animal-like determination for survival in life.

The night wore on with the enemy searching the ground with meticulous insistency. A ghostly unreal night crowded steeply upward in wearing monotony until it fell back on us in a great wave of fatigue. At 0420 he put over his last heavy shoot and then lapsed into intermittent fire. We slept until daylight.

*   *   *

Next morning everyone looked a little older and had little to say. The cook filled our mess tins and we wandered off out of the rain somewhere and ate in silence. We were keen to learn what had happened during that frightful night. We could only piece together fragments of the picture. The most persistent rumour was that the Seaforths had withdrawn to the south side of the Moro, from their critical position below San Leonardo. This left us with two widely separated and grimly-held bridgeheads: the Pats with the British Tanks in Roatti, and the Hastie-Pees on Punta Acquabella at the estuary of the river. What seemed certain was that we were all just a little punch-drunk and groggy from lack of sleep and, although no one admitted this to be the case, conversation was fitful and lacked the spirit of two days back.

I had little desire to paint, but I returned to yesterday's location to look over the situation. My inertia vanished as four M.E.'s broke cloud behind the town. The valley burst

into sudden deafening life as everything went up at the
raiders. Bofors, Orlikons, Brens, tracers laced the sky and
black ack-ack bursts surrounded the visitors. As they ended
their screaming dive and turned out to sea, bombs started
down. Though they have only a few hundred feet to fall
an eternity passes as they slip swiftly and silently to their
target. All eyes follow that mathematical curve of destruction
with helpless anguish. The planes disappeared over the
Adriatic as the detonations rocked San Vito and towering
columns of yellowish dust rose in the vicinity of the bursts.
Under a lengthening pall of blue-grey smoke, a brisk fire
crackled away in the town. It happens so quickly; possibly
ninety seconds had elapsed from the time I first saw the
planes until they vanished over the sea. I glanced about me
and turned once more to my painting.

It was not so much the recurring distractions of the
situation as the physical and nervous exhaustion that dulled
my perceptive faculties that morning, the effect of the bombing, the thought of the human losses to be learned later. With
laborious effort, I started to paint. For me painting has
always been a quiet contemplative communion between me
and whatever may have set my creative faculties in motion.
Today I was painting, but somehow it seemed a mechanical
act, subconsciously motivated, detached from me completely.
I saw the washes settle on the paper; they behaved with surprising agreement of purpose, and gradually the image of
San Vito took shape, framed by the cane-brake surrounding
me. But for me it was not inspired painting; it contained
none of the feeling of holocaust which I associated with the
location and of which I was most painfully conscious; it was
empty, drained of content, even as I myself. The contemplative
mood was impossible.

As I worked the fury of the bombardment opened up
with renewed vigour. A constant stream of trucks descended
the winding hill, from the town to the Bailey that took them
across the river. As I looked up, a shell struck squarely into
the column, hiding the vehicles momentarily in a grey smudge

of cordite smoke. Out of this a truck staggered crazily, its
front wheels crashing through the guard rail. The column
stopped, drivers running to the ditches for cover. The diverted
truck hung miraculously suspended over the verge of the road.
When it was apparent that it was not an air attack, the
column resumed its movement and soon I saw the Provost
attending the damaged vehicle. Incidents such as these were
a violent accompaniment to painting. I remembered an artist
friend in Toronto who could not paint because of the noise
of a dog barking. But artists had painted war before, even
if not from inside the storm itself as we were attempting to
do. I felt equal to the task, in fact I felt supremely aware.
But today I was tired; what I needed was sleep.

*   *   *

Mid-afternoon we heard that 1st Brigade had been
ordered to establish a deep bridgehead across the Moro by
capturing San Leonardo. 2nd Brigade, with the Calgary
and Ontario Tank Regiments, were to pass through at first
light, the objective being to capture and consolidate on the
crossroads, a dramatic location later known to all as the
Berardi crossroads. This looked to be a formidable task,
but if it were successful it might be possible for us to by-pass
Ortona.

By last light fantastic rumours had spread regarding
the scale of tomorrow's effort to get 1st Brigade across the
river. No one knew the time of the attack but it was said
that the Navy was to help too. Once more we were buoyed
up with hope.

*   *   *

Darkness came at half-past four. As daylight faded, we
prepared ourselves for the ordeal of the night. We had moved
our bivy from the ploughed grove where the mud now reached
half-way up my rubber boots. Our new location was in the
lee of a clay shelf, drier and, we hoped, more secure. Ogilvie
had brought down "Whitey" to visit us and we reviewed the

situation and speculated on the possibilities inherent in tomorrow's rumoured action. Ogilvie had known Captain Whitehead all through the Sicilian campaign; before the war he had been a Don at Cambridge where he taught Romance Languages. He was muddy and tired like ourselves, overwhelmed by the refugee problem which appeared to be his special concern.

Except for our own batteries and the steady noise of heavy supply trucks grinding up the hill on low gear, the enemy was contenting himself with what appeared to be idle or harassing fire. By that I mean that shells were falling up and down the valley with no seemingly fixed purpose except to keep us awake. The sky was clearing, following a day of rain, and with the atmospheric clarity we could distinctly hear the distant whump as the guns fired, followed a few seconds later by the eerie whistle as the missile approached over its trajectory. Then the detonation shook the valley and we casually estimated the location of the burst. These were lighter shells, like twenty-five pounders; he must have a battery of S.P.'s limbering up on us tonight.

The night was starkly clear, moonlit and mild; the shelling as devastating as ever. The first long shoot lasted until midnight. The targets were the same, the supply road and the Bailey bridge, the mediums in the valley and the field batteries, both behind the town and between us and the Moro. A tumultuous night, ghostly and unreal, under the spectral light descending from that lidless gorgon eye, staring unmoved from the sky; a cruel laughing witness, detached, existing in cosmic silence, out of the reach of lead and steel, glaring down on this shattered landscape.

Toward five in the morning the bombardment eased up a bit and those who could relax slept. The dawn was chilly and there was a heavy dew as the sun shot up into a cloudless sky. The morning and early afternoon were crowded with air action. Four Focke-Wulfs appeared early, flying at an immense height, with long vapour trails streaming behind like bridal veils, and surrounded with the deadly confetti of ack-ack. No doubt they were gathering information on our lines of communication.

Far more exciting were the flights of Kittyhawks and Mitchells that were strafing the German positions across the Moro. They sailed in in formations of six, peeled off, dived, machine gunned, bombed, swooped up and were gone. Surrounded by black ack-ack, it seemed miraculous that they were not hit. They were, of course, from time to time, but I never witnessed it.

There was only one topic at Brigade this morning, the barrage and attack this afternoon. Zero was notified as 1530 hours, 1st Brigade leading off, the 48th Highlanders crossing the Moro and attacking San Leonardo from the west, the Royal Canadian Regiment from the east, through the bridge-head now held by the Hastings and Prince Edward Regiment. Tension grew as zero approached.

Ken Cottam arrived with his jeep about two o'clock and invited Ogilvie and me to go forward with him. We left the highway where it branches off toward San Appolinare and cut across an olive grove to a hedgerow where we harboured and demobilized the vehicle. Then, creeping and crawling along the shadow of the hedge, we reached the southern brink of the valley.

We lay prone and still on the skyline. The trembling grasses that separated us from what we saw, offered a very ineffectual screen from enemy eyes across the valley. Although it was December, the afternoon sun was pleasantly warm; nearby a lizard basked on a stone, still, like ourselves, except for the rapid pulsing of his soft belly; a lark's song descended from the zenith. We had brought entrenching tools and started to dig, but the stoney ground was relentlessly hard and the task called for more exposure than we cared to risk. So there we lay quietly in cover, looking about us for a convenient shellhole in which we might shelter from whatever might come our way.

Except for one or two sinister reminders, the scene was one of tranquil pastoral beauty, a quiet beauty that had remained unchanged since Theodoric's time possibly, or even before. To our right was the headland that marked the estuary of the river, now held by the Hastings and Prince Edward Regiment, beyond it, the empty Adriatic, shimmering in the late autumnal sunshine. The valley below was typical of the water courses that channel this coastal plain, two hundred feet perhaps to its floor, a thousand yards across. At the bottom, a muddy stream, high at this season, meandered through shrubs and vetches and occasional clumps of willow. The concrete span that had carried the road had been demolished. In front could be seen two Sherman tanks, harboured behind the willows. The reverse slope, with its burden of olive, rose in gentle folds to its crest, the highway snaking up its flank toward San Leonardo. The plain beyond undulated off to the horizon with its plotted fertility and cube-like white farm buildings. Ortona gleamed attractively in the distance, clustered about the cupola of San Tomasso.

Our cockloft was a grandstand seat for inferno. As the minutes ticked away, insects buzzed in the sunshine; a magpie, followed by its pendulous tail, flitted in deep swags across our line of vision. Five minutes to zero . . . An idle shell whined across the valley; the horizon wavered in the cordial-like heat haze. December at home . . . there might even be snow at this date, certainly in some parts of Canada. Here Monte Amaro wedged up into the warm sky in a blue silhouette. One minute . . . We adjusted our helmets; the metal was hot and the chin strap difficult to adjust.

Then inferno broke loose; the earth trembled with cataclysmic shock. Instantly the pastoral valley became a valley of death. From its fertile groves sprang the instant and terrible orchids of death. The first impact was of sound, gigantic and preposterous sound. One was shuttled from warm sunlight into the roaring darkness of an endless tunnel. It battered and pounded the eardrums from all sides. We lay stunned and fearful, clawing the earth, as flights of frightened birds crossed the valley and passed over our heads to a relative safety. Before our eyes sprang the grey-blue flowers of death, withering instantly in the breeze, to form a concealing veil of sulphurous vapour, struggling to hide the agony of that clamorous garden.

Two creeping figures appeared on the crest to our right, wearing necklaces of ammunition, the bright casings glinting in the sunshine. They levelled their weapons, waiting for the beaters to flush the game. Beyond them, concealed in a coppice, was a machine gun crew of the Saskatchewan Light Infantry, waiting like instrumentalists for the down-beat that would bring them into the score they knew so well.

No sound of speech or movement could be heard above the infernal dissonance; all was lost in the tumult of its fury. The target pattern soon became clear: neat rectangles were searched and scorched with fire, the finger pointing here and then there. Soon they all fitted together with diabolic accuracy, like the parts of a gigantic puzzle. When the assembly was complete, all that the eye could encompass had been burned with fire. The valley was gone, hidden in an opaque cloud of acrid cordite. One was possessed of a great fatigue, a throbbing of the temples. What a dreadful monotony it was, of key, of tempo, of colour, of purpose and effect.

At 1635 hours, with this vast percussion still continuing, the Saskatchewan Light Infantry went into action, their heavy machine guns spraying the enemy positions with penetrating bursts like pneumatic drills. To our astonishment, the enemy replied with the even faster falsetto of the Schmeisser. How could humans survive such a barrage? Why were they not helpless inarticulate blobs of quivering jelly?

But the finer and more deadly phases of the duel were now approaching. Men were emerging from deep hiding, like sullen beasts, shaken, baited and desperate, crawling in cover in the vapour-filled valley, jockeying with death mid this fearful cacaphony. At 1645 hours the enemy artillery opened up on the line of the river bed with heavy seventeen centimetre shells, great towering jagged bursts that soon engulfed the bridge, swallowed up the harboured tanks, and took over the noise-making like a chorus of operatic baritones. The final ear-splitting phase was awful to witness. What of those men? Were they battle-wise and again secure in cover? Nothing, it seemed to us, could survive that fire as it tossed earth and trees high in the air. Yet down there were Canadian Engineers, ready to sweep the fords and get the bridge across; on their start line were the 48th, waiting for the quiet, "All right fellahs, let's go!"

We lay prone and still on a skyline. The trembling grasses that separated us from what we saw offered a very ineffectual screen from observant eyes behind the enemy line. The battle raged all about us; enemy shells screamed through the dusk just above our heads and we could hear heavy slamming bursts behind us.

We regained the jeep and drove the mile back to Brigade Headquarters, shaken and dazed.

The night that followed was the most hellish of all; Ogilvie and I spent it largely in the slit trench, tense, helpless, frightened and tired. Everywhere destruction and disintegration: shattered buildings, mutilated trees, a spectral landscape of heaped-up fleshless bones, jostled by concussion and blast in a hideous monotonous dance macabre. Such was the new tempestuous world of cataclysm and shock we had inherited.

Our frayed nerves were as taut as zither strings, twanging in wild dissonance in response to the unreal violence of the night. We were conscious of blood pulsing heavily through arteries and veins, the heart thumping in the breast like a separate entity, detached and independent of one's body, enduring its own struggle, the eardrums like timpani unmercifully hammered by a thousand percussionists. Jesus Christ! How long can it go on? How long can this frail human mechanism stand it?

*   *   *

We had stayed two further dreadful days at Brigade, following the attack across the Moro on the eighth. Then

CANADIAN FIELD GUNS NEAR ORTONA.

PIAZZA PLEBISCITO, ORTONA.

we had received a signal from the Camp Commandant, requiring us to return to the Division. We collected our equipment and, with a certain sadness, thanked the Staff Captain and said good-bye. Somehow or other we felt we were walking out in the middle of a job. Although we were happy at the thought of a break, it did not seem right that we should be singled out for this privilege.

Back at Division we discovered the reason for the signal: Captain L. P. Harris had arrived from the U.K. and Captain W. A. Ogilvie was to return to London forthwith. Ogilvie and I were delighted to see Lawren Harris whom we had known for years and, when Hughes appeared, Hist. Sec. took on the appearance of old home week. However, we had little time to celebrate the event. Ogilvie was to leave for Naples next morning and, being short of paper and artists' supplies, I was to go with him to make good these shortages and shepherd the vehicle there and back.

Drizzling rain and the dark skies had a healing, soothing effect on our jangled nerves. The supply road was crowded and as northbound vehicles had the right of way, we were halted frequently. Casalbordino looked somehow appealing in the soft grey light, with shining wet streets and just the semblance of a returning normality. It was nearly four o'clock when we entered Termoli, and with rain and overcast it was already growing dark. Filled with an abounding optimism, we went straight to the Town Major to request accommodation. His deputy was a rather austere looking English type. He glanced disapprovingly at our muddy feet and clothing and suggested the staging camp at the entrance to the town. We were a little annoyed by this peremptory instruction and hurried off to Amgot to have it set aside. To our horror we ran into more English officers there, completely uninterested in our problem. Once the official sources of accommodation had been investigated, nothing more could be done in Termoli, so we reluctantly returned to the staging camp. As we had expected, it was just another ploughed field with more, deeper, and even stickier mud than we had been accustomed to.

We reported in at the muddy orderly room, were assigned to a tent erected over a morass, and ate in a mud-floored marquee which sounded and felt like walking on sticky fly-paper.

*   *   *

We reached Naples before night-fall next day and went directly to the office of the Town Major. After arranging for Fiddler's accommodation at Capodimonte, we were assigned to the Albergo Sirena on the Piazza Garibaldi. We were in a proper frame of mind to accept with uncritical enthusiasm the modest amenities of this typical railway hotel. An ageing facchino helped us upstairs with our dunnage to Room 51. After crouching in a wet slit-trench for ten days, one is overwhelmed by the sight of a bed, any bed. There were two in this room, twin beds. Without removing our trench coats, we flopped onto the beds, shouting exaggerated expressions of sheer joy. The facchino looked on incredulously; it must have been a rare experience for him to witness such unreserved enthusiasm for the Sirena's furnishings.

We sent him off for wine and water, for although there was a wash-basin in the room, a sign warned us that the taps ran for only two hours each morning. We unpacked, beside ourselves with the delight of being in a dry lighted room. Simone returned with water and two bottles of Gragnano vini dell Gaudio. He called it Spumante and charged for it as such. We murmured not a word of protest, although it was obviously not Spumante but tasted instead like carbonated apple cider.

Nothing, absolutely nothing, could have destroyed our overwhelming sense of blissful happiness that night. Even the certain knowledge that we were to be parted in the next day or so did not disturb us. We did not give it a thought. We had escaped, escaped fortuitously, from the tensions and fatigue of a desperate battle, a battle that was beginning to wear us thin.

Naples was mellow under the pale warm sunshine of winter, a warm dusty mellowness. One of the older colours in an artist's palette is an antimonate of lead, known as Giallo di Napoli. This morning there seemed to exist a chromatic affinity between that pigment and the atmosphere of the city. Within this hazy penumbra walked thousands of citizens.

The darkness of the Vittoria tunnel brought us out into the sunshine of the Riviera di Chiaia (the Riviera of Light) with its sub-tropical botanical gardens, the aquarium, and the vast expanse of the bay. Our eyes swept the scene avidly before we turned up one of the shadowy side streets. The Canadian Section of Allied Force Headquarters was situated in the Rione Sirignano, in what appeared to be a tall block of flats. They may have been suites of offices, certainly it was a complicated maze and the problem of finding Lieut. Colonel Tow was a baffling one.

Ogilvie appeared sometime later, wreathed in smiles. The outcome of the interview seemed to please him and indeed it did sound exciting. He was to leave by plane on the 16th for Algiers and from that point he was to proceed to England by the first boat. He was delighted with a prospect that might mean his being in London for Christmas with all that that implied. The only hitch was that he must report to the A.A.D.A.G. daily so that the precise time of the flight could be advised.

Back in the sunshine again, we drove up the delightful Rampe di Posillipo, debating the propriety of my holding the vehicle in Naples until Thursday, the day of the flight. We paused at a little cafe whose name intrigued us and where, we thought, it might be easier to consider a plan.

"Piccolo Paradiso" was empty at that mid-morning hour. The view from its window overlooked the dramatic fatal beauty of the bay. We ordered caffe expresso and cognac and settled down to talk and enjoy the remarkable scene. Quiet sunshine lay gently on the volcanic crags of Ischia. Sky and sea seemed suffused in an ephemeral haze in which floated the

twin peaks of Capri and the peaceful headlands of Massalu-
breuse and Sorrento. A white veil rose from the formidable
bulk of Vesuvius and gave scale, gigantic scale, to this vast
panorama. It was decided that if tomorrow's interview with
the A.A.D.A.G. confirmed Colonel Tow's plan, I should stay
until Thursday; this balmy December day and the seductive
charm of the region did much to convince us, not so much of
the wisdom, but of the undoubted therapeutic value of this
decision.

*   *   *

Following lunch we went out through the depressing ruins
of Portici, found the Autostrada, and made our way to
Pompeii. (Except for one section of about four hundred yards,
the Autostrada had escaped serious damage.) There were
some huge bomb craters beside the road, but the highway
itself was intact except for one short section.

Pompeii was peaceful and lovely in the afternoon sunshine
and, what appealed to us most of all, it was practically
deserted. We entered the ruins through the Porta Marina,
the gateway facing the sea. A bomb had brought down some
of the structure and we were obliged to climb over a pile of
masonry and rubble, high enough for us to touch the soffit
of the arched tunnel. The spectacle of a city, buried in lapilli
and ashes in the first century, bombed and redamaged in the
twentieth, was fantastic. Anti-aircraft gun sites were scattered
through the ruins; the incongruity of coming upon a carefully
camouflaged Bofors, poking up menacingly out of the peristyle
of a Greco-Roman villa, had all the shocking force of continental surrealism.

The Strada dell Marina possesses the sepulchral stillness
of Mount Pleasant Cemetery, less that chlorophyl accompaniment of grass and trees. A broken apron of steps leads
to an empty podium. Two lonely and desolate Corinthian
shafts frame Vesuvius. A heavy meaningless entablature rests
uncertainly on a series of cracked and eroded columns. A
bronze Apollo stares blindly across the Forum, casting a long

attenuated shadow. Empty perspectives stretched nostalgically
in every direction, echoing to our hobnails as we walked along
the rutted causeway of the Viccolo di Mercurio toward the
house of the Vettii. The Vettii were undoubtedly wealthy
men of rank; their villa must have been a superb example of
luxurious domestic building during the last decades of the
city's life, with splendid mural painting and a charming garden.
Today it is one of those evocative ruins, complete enough
for one to recreate its past magnificence. A room off the
peristyle had been hit by a bomb or a shell and debris was
scattered about the fresco which depicts the Punishment of
Dirce. Dirce's agonizing expression appeared to lament this
new violence, rather than the efforts of Zethus and Amphion
to tie her to the tail of a wild bull. On the west wall of the
smaller atrium we found a charming shrine of Lararium, with
a Lewis Carol serpent wriggling across the foreground,
beneath a priestess accompanied by dancing lares. The garden
appeared neglected, though it is said to contain flora and
shrubs which originally flourished there, papyrus, acanthus,
roses, ivy, palms, and oleander.

Out again in the disinterred city, Ogilvie and I picked up
a stray guide on the Strada Consulare. Though he had very
little English we made it clear to him that we wanted to reach
the Villa die Misteri by the quickest route as it was already
growing late.

The Villa of the Mysterie is thought to have been built
for a patrician family in the third century B.C. Between that
date and the eruption which buried the city, it had been altered
and enlarged to a residence of palatial size. We were not so
interested in the size and structural features of the villa as we
were in the fact that about a century before the final disaster
the then owner had commissioned an artist to paint a great
fresco in one of the rooms. Although many of the Pompeian
frescoes are obviously painted by artisans, even decorators,
this particular painting is by an artist of outstanding ability.
The subject matter is concerned with the Dionysiac mysteries,

pagan rites during which brides are initiated into the service
of the Gods by submitting to certain secret experiences.

We entered over a foot-bridge and found the interior
darker than we would have wished. The room which contains
the great fresco was indeed mysterious, even sinister, in the
half light. The figures loomed out of the walls with an
enigmatic suggestiveness that chilled one momentarily. We
fell silent, as if under a spell, as the ecstatic mood of the
actors became apparent; they were all actors, hieretic actors,
except for the candidate and the witnesses. The action ran
around the wall in a sequence of tableaux of extraordinary
naturalism; an old Silenus sang and played a lyre with en-
raptured feeling; Ogilvie called my attention to the dramatic
figure of a frightened woman with a billowing scarf raised
above her head, starting back, almost pleading with the
winged female demon who scourged the kneeling candidate.
We were impressed with the moving character of the composition, the delicate drawing, the fine three-dimensional tonal
painting, the pale harmonies of colour set off against a
panelled background of Pompeian red. A beautiful nude
Bacchante danced in some orgiastic trance. The figures of
Dionysus and Ariadne had been damaged, but enough remained of the tableau in which they occur to reconstruct its
composition. Unquestionably a feeling of profound mystery
emanates from this remarkable painting. As we walked back
to the Humber we pondered why it had happened to be
painted in a private residence, a residence rather than a temple.

*   *   *

We had been wakened early by cries from a nearby
street market, and by Anna the chambermaid, filling the wash
basin with hot water and serving us a cup of tea. These
almost-forgotten luxuries of civilized living cheered us no end.
We made light of the necessity of our both having to shave
in the same basin of water, which was not nearly as serious

a matter as the complete absence of water in the cistern of the men's toilet.

Later at 1st Echelon Ogilvie reported, as ordered, to the A.A.D.A.G., Captain Glendenning. Evidently the Captain was in possession of security information because his first purpose was to discourage any further thought of the proposed flight to Algiers. At "Movement," Major Simmons put Ogilvie on the nominal roll for the next sailing, the date and hour a security matter. "Just report here every day. We will let you know in lots of time." It was obviously not going to be tomorrow or the next day.

We had given Fiddler the day off, so we took the delightful walk along the Via Caracciolo. The sun poured down with the warmth of an Indian Summer's day as we moved in and out of the shadows of magnificent royal palms. I had decided, as a result of the morning's interview, to return to the Division next morning. With the date of Ogilvie's departure such an uncertainty, there was no longer any valid reason for my holding the vehicle. The Via Parthenope was bathed in dusty sunshine and the spectacle of the Neopolitan luxury hotels, standing empty and neglected, seemed preposterous.

We strolled on past the naval arsenal and, looking out over the harbour, marvelled at the remarkable engineering feat which had restored its usefulness so quickly, following the destructive ingenuity lavished on it by the enemy sappers. The Piazza Plebiscito, a wide cobbled area, was crowded with military vehicles; dust and paper flew fitfully about in the breezy sunshine. A violent orange drink was being offered at tiny glistering stalls, festooned with glowing fruit set off against its own green leaves. Hunger vitiated urchins, with large bright eyes and an aggressive manner, proffered caramello and a horribly sticky-looking nut fudge.

The troops in town are nearly all from 5th Army, as is the vehicular traffic, going in both directions. Naples is, of course, in the Fifth Army sector as well as being A.F.H.Q. It is to be expected that troops seen are overwhelmingly American, a gay, exuberant, well-turned-out lot, and the friendliest relations exist between them and the Canadians. A lot of good-natured "kibitzing" goes on, in which we fare far better than say the British or the New Zealanders. In fact there is little difference between us, except the uniforms we wear, how we wear them, the accommodations we are assigned, the folding money we carry, the rations we draw, and our disinclination to talk about exploits in the field.

At the cartoleria I was able to stock up on excellent Fabriano papers, Hardmuth charcoals, sepias and sanguine. But they had neither brushes nor paints suitable to my purpose.

*   *   *

The air inside the old San Carlo Opera House smelt of stale cigar smoke, face powder, and carpet dust. The vast rococo auditorium, although neglected, still retained much of the theatrical splendour of its magnificent past. It had escaped obvious damage, although I was told that backstage it was somewhat of a shambles and that sets, properties and many of the costumes were no more.

Two costumed footmen, right out of King Bomba's court, parted the curtains and revealed possibly the largest orchestra we had ever seen, with countless stands of violins, scores of other instruments, rank after rank of bass viols in the background. Maestro Pasquariello faced the audience, which stood as the opening bars of "The Star-spangled Banner" spread through the house. At its conclusion we were about to be seated when the strains of the Internationale started up, to be followed endlessly, so it seemed, by the national anthem of each of the Allied Nations, concluding with "God Save the King." National identities having thus been honoured, we at last resumed our seats and settled to enjoy what followed.

The principal work on the programme was Tchaikovsky's Piano Concerto, Opus 23. Although the work abounds with theatrically facile passages and brooding sentimentality, we lapped it up as if it were nectar. Gentle tremulous phrases passed into an eager romanticism and then on to strident headlong crescendoes. The dark fury of winter, wind sighing in bare trees, miming dancers on carpets of flowers. Flora, pale and fragile as a gentian, singing a gentle melody in a thin sweet voice as Zephyr stirred a cloud of butterflies. The tall, the blonde, the elegant; the stern dark-cloaked figure moving in the shadow, biding his time as the soldier mounts and rides off in the darkness. I had wondered if we should ever hear again, but apparently nothing had been lost. The thunder of gunfire had passed and was forgotten. The responses thought to have been deadened were intact and alive, and life was good.

*   *   *

With the realization that the party was over, we returned to the Sirena for dinner. We were going our separate ways in the morning. Who knew where or when we should meet again? It was an existence in which self-determination played a very small part. But any deep-welling currents of apprehension which may have surged within were completely suppressed as we finished our drink and made our way to the dining-room.

We had foreseen the importance of this evening and, earlier in the day, had conspired with our waiter to obtain for us two "black market" veal steaks with a suitable quantity of "Vesuvio" red wine. Nothing could have pleased his sardonic character more than to have been taken into confidence on such a clandestine deal. He raised his eyebrow reassuringly as we appeared at the table. I must say he had done full justice to our wishes, of course at a price. The round ball of fish was elegantly named "Trance di pesce ballets" and the steaks, although thin, were richly spiced and enormously good. We sat a long time over oranges and coffee and it was late before we started to pack.

*   *   *

Fiddler stood by the Humber at the curb, his head and beret wreathed in sunshine, the same gentle sunshine that had blessed us ever since our arrival in Naples, and in a moment we were off, up the Corsa Garibaldi in a trail of golden dust, and Will, of course, on his way to pay his daily compliment to the A.A.D.A.G. It was two hundred miles to Divisional H.Q., a journey which would take us over the mountains from the Campagna to the Tavolerie plains and then north along the Adriatic.

The climb up to Montesarchio was painfully slow. Trapped between two three-tonners, we simply crawled up the long gradients. As we approached Avellino, through that extraordinary tunnel of ilex trees, it became clear that if this traffic congestion continued we should barely reach Foggia during daylight. Convoys persisted. By 1400 hours we came to a dead stop in an insoluble jam on the narrow road through Ariano-Irpino. There was nothing to be done; we could not even leave the vehicle to attend to creature comforts. Reaching Main 40 was now out of the question as a daylight objective; we had covered only sixty miles in five hours. It looked more like Foggia, unless we drove all night. However, we eventually did get going and Ariano proved to be the end of our troubles. Where the convoys went was no concern of ours. We descended the precipitous curving road down through the valley of the Torrente Cervaro, an impressive valley recalling the Manning National Park in British Columbia, and on down a traffic-free road to the rolling foothills and out onto the wide coastal plain around Foggia. There we stopped only long enough to take on gas before continuing on while we had the road to ourselves. Soon after passing through San Severo the sun set gloriously behind the mountains and darkness quickly fell.

*   *   *

The battle for Ortona raged with demoniac fury. Day after hellish day men clubbed and smashed one another at close quarters for desperate short-range objectives, a farmhouse, an irrigation ditch, a bit of rising ground, a coulee,

edging forward in quick staggering bounds, crawling breathlessly in the muck, through writhing vineyards, dragging
the mortars, the bombs, the brens, the piats, the grenades;
rallying around the tanks as they roared out of harbour at
last light; flanking the position under covering fire, rushing
it in the half light, through sheets of blinding flame, hurling
the grenades and closing in through lacerating, pounding,
light-stabbed darkness; stumbling, cursing, tearing at the wire,
alert with the horrible necessity of killing. A deafening actinic
flash. The tank heaves like a ship at sea under the impact,
and then comes to rest, immobilized and helpless. A silhouette
staggers forward, firing from the hip, and disappears into
the censoring darkness. The attack falters as its fire-power
declines. One and two on the bren direct covering fire as the
survivors retire to consolidate and prepare for the inevitable
counter-attack.

Sam Hughes told me something of the furious succession
of actions which had taken us a mile and a half beyond the
Moro in the past six days. It had been laboriously, painfully
slow-going in that tenacious mud. The enemy were said to be
moving down a great number of guns and reinforcements
into this coastal area, determined to pin us down. Every yard
gained or lost has been paid for in mounting casualties. It
appears that we are astride the lateral road on our left flank
and command a ridge overlooking Ortona, which lies two
miles beyond. But the enemy still occupies the town and
holds a number of heavily defended draws and fortified houses
which intervene. One of the most stubbornly defended of these
locations lies just beyond the crest of the ridge in the deep
furrow that carries the Torrente Saraceni, known to us all as
"The Gully." Two Canadian battalions have suffered heavy
losses attempting to reduce this resistance. Just two days ago
elements of the Royal 22nd had accomplished this outflanking
manœuvre by mounting a daring attack along the axis of the
lateral road. In face of heavy resistance, and in a desperate
hand-to-hand effort they had captured a fortified farm house
known as the *"Casa Berardi."* At the time, we were not

aware of the heroic part played in this battering engagement
by Captain Paul Triquet of the Royal 22nd Regiment. It was
much later that we learned of his personal courage and
resourceful leadership at the Berardi Farm action and that
he had been nominated to receive the highest award in the
service.

Every effort was being bent toward the major objective
of clearing the enemy from Ortona with the port facilities
intact, if possible. The liberation of the town would be a
moral victory, but if we could make use of its harbour, following the clearance, the victory would be a strategic one as well.
The atmosphere at Divisional headquarters was tense. The
grave determined faces of operational officers reflected the
grim malignant nature of the battle we were joined in. They
were resolute faces from which the earlier buoyancy had
temporarily vanished. There was little or no small talk around
the messes; conversation centred around the ebb and flow of
battle. We had three brigades up, no reserves; expenditures
in men, equipment and ammunition were high, replacements
disappointingly low. And then there was the weather and the
exasperating conditions it brought on. Added to all this was
the fanatical character of enemy resistance. Lots of room for
sleepless concern for those who did the thinking and made
the decisions.

The site of the headquarters did little to sustain the
waning spirit. We were concealed under nets and garnish
in a flattish olive grove that had been ground and churned
into a depressing morass of extraordinarily plastic mud.
Water-filled ruts, two feet deep, made movement in any
direction an amphibious operation. The air was charged
with the concussion of gun-fire which rose in deafening chorus
from artillery sites crowded all about us. One hideous new
voice of disturbing power rose above the others, which Hughes
told me came from a battery of high muzzle velocity 3.7
inch ack-ack guns. From our position they were hidden, but
their presence was loudly announced by a vicious stunning
slam each time they were fired.

Hughes looked tired and peaked. He had been working hard, gathering reports at both Brigade and Battalion levels: I knew something of what that meant.

The growing pressures of the battle crowded all about us. There was no escape from the vast declamatory thunder which shook the plain and the groves of olive with titanic violence. A raw chill drizzle descended from a dense wrack of darkening cloud which hid the ancient sea and the fierce grandeur of the Miella, bringing inexpressible misery to all. L.A.D.'s and gargantuan recovery vehicles hauled and winched at bogged transport in a grim battle of their own, a battle against the elements, a battle to keep the schedules of movement operative which, for sheer physical struggle rivalled the efforts of the enemy to frustrate our plans.

It was difficult to pursue my own work either outdoors or in. Papers were limp and cockled; washes simply refused to dry. On the second day following my return, as darkness fell, Sam Hughes returned to the tent, drawing hopelessly on his pipe with the bowl upsidedown. We were ready for the next bound, if this bloody weather would only settle a bit. 1st Brigade was all set to put in a strong artillery and tank-supported attack in the morning. The objective was to straddle the crossroads east of the Casa Berardi and consolidate beyond it. The great "softening up" shoot was to begin at 0800 hours, named with delicate irony "Morning Glory." Since we had been warned not to proceed beyond San Leonardo, I resolved to cover some aspect of this artillery preparation.

We spent a restless night; enemy gunners were very active. For my part, I lay wakefully apprehensive in my blankets, tracing the deployment and movement of the S.P.'s. Earlier in the night I had heard laughter and cursing from a nearby tent where the L.O.'s were playing poker, but their gaming had long since ended.

It was still dark as Hughes and I slopped down through the mud to the steamy warmth of the mess tent next morning. The drizzle had ceased and the heavy cloud strata had risen considerably. Following coffee and hot something it was

obvious that the day would be overcast, but at least the rain
was holding off. Layers of coiling mist made eerie fantasy
about the twisted olives and the lacy textures of the nets
glistened with moisture. Firing was of a desultory character,
the calm before the storm.

Hughes needed the Humber to go to Brigade but agreed
to drop me and my equipment in the Medium area, sited just
south of San Vito. Lieut. Evans greeted me at the command
post of "C" for Charlie Troop, 4th Medium Regiment, Royal
Artillery. The mediums were Corps weapons and, of course,
the 1st Canadian Division was then under command of the
5th British Corps of the 8th Army. I made my reconnaissance
and selected an exposed location immediately behind one of
the gun-sites.

The imagery of a gun-site, detached from its purpose and
environment, is a strange fusion of machined surfaces, kinetic
routines, and the delicate transparent tracery of the nets. The
weapon itself stood silently awaiting zero, a monumental
machine of devastating power, its long barrel thrust menacingly upward and outward like some prehistoric bronto-
saurus peering from its cocoon-like cave for some sign of
prey. The crew busied themselves with fuses, charges and
ammunition, which stood about in vast stacks. The floor of
the shallow gun pit was paved with loose brick, round which
the mud oozed like fresh mortar. A wall of sandbags and
sand-filled charge boxes formed a protective parapet, while
above a canopy of nets and garnish spread a delicate mem-
branous web of camouflage. The five minute signal had gone
and the one minute was expected momentarily. The helmeted
numbers took their stations and all was in readiness to launch
"Morning Glory."

The lanyard was pulled and the gun recoiled behind the
monstrous muzzle blast. A flower-like, pink-edged flame of
instant blooming gave place to shocking, numbing sound and
a concussion that jumped my equipment clear off the ground.
Guns in every direction gouted flame with furious energy.
One felt suspended helplessly in some dense exhausting element

where sound, and sound only, existed. The first concentrated phase of the barrage was mercifully brief.

I had begun my drawing before the firing started; it was quite impossible for me to proceed during that first phase. Then it scaled back to a timed schedule and I resumed my work with a wary eye on the sergeant.

As one looked about that sodden grove and saw the flame jets burning the gloom of that dark morning, one could imagine the shells patterning in concentration on the target area, the attackers breaking cover and following closely under that destructive curtain, fountains of wet spoil, shattered trees, masonry and shrieking fragmentation filling the darkened air, the armour finding difficulty in manoeuvring to advantage in the boggy spoil, slithering to a standstill in heavy mud, delaying the momentum of the infantry attack and its balanced impact against the timing of the barrage. But of course we heard nothing during that noisy morning of the attack's success or failure.

The first phase of "Morning Glory" over, the mediums lapsed into a relative silence. Lieut. Evans left the command post and picked his way through the guck to report his guns, moving carefully from one site to the next in a pair of muddy waders. Finally he came smilingly my way and invited me to eat my lunch at the post when I could spare the time.

About this time the first of several ranging air-bursts blossomed darkly overhead. Everyone regarded these suspiciously. They could mean trouble, but very often they did not. In this case they did and the first pattern of four came in well announced over by the road on the left. I mused that it might be the road they were interested in and proceeded with my painting as if nothing had happened. Then without warning a sickening whump crashed somewhere behind us. I felt the blast and shock of it like the breath of a tornado on my neck and back. Instantly I was lying on the floor of the gun pit, trembling like a frightened hart, conscious only of the presence of imminent peril and the profanity of the Midland gun numbers. Several other sharp bursts filled the immediate air with sound and fury. I turned my head and looked back. A sluggish breeze raised the corner of the paper on my easel, thirty feet away. Beside the easel stood my stool and the charge box containing my other equipment. A waft of bluish smoke drifted across the park, smelling not unlike the burning stumps of fire-crackers. Victoria Day in the evening, pinwheels and Roman candles, children following the soaring flight of a rocket in the fading light, the odour of melancholy and memory, like the distant sound in conch shells . . . Beyond, three blankets stirred languidly on a line strung between two olive trees. The angel had flown close; we had heard the beating wings.

Laughter spread to all of us in the pit. "Cheer up! You never hear the one that gets you," observed an unseen voice. But no one moved, the muddy pit still had its attraction for those of us who valued survival. Then "Bastard! Look at my bloody blankets!" The heads all lifted toward the blankets which still hung quietly on their line. As they stirred slowly, daylight could be seen shining brightly through the fresh tears. Still lying prone we were convulsed with nervous laughter when "Take Post" was shouted. Immediately danger vanished, or so it seemed, and everyone sprang into action as range, elevation, and charge orders were loudly repeated. I puddle-hopped back to my easel, looking hopefully for more convenient cover.

*   *   *

The battle fury increased hour by hour, pyramiding up and up in rising crescendo, a wild barbaric extravaganza of uncompromising violence. We had been warned of a move but no one knew when it would be. "Just keep yourselves packed and ready to be on your way in twenty minutes." The crossroads were in our hands and we were patrolling to the outskirts of the town; optimism was rising again as the Canadians closed in on their stubborn quarry.

The weather alternated between steady rain and occasional pale diluted sunshine. On the day following "Morning Glory," d'Arcy Doherty gave us the co-ordinates for the heavy ack-ack battery and Harris and I spent the better part of two days with these nerve-shattering weapons. Their original role had been the ack-ack defence of the Sangro crossing, but during this critical phase of the attack they were taking on field targets the same as everyone else.

Lawren Harris, Jr., is now my companion in most of these experiences. He looks older. I have known him since he was a teen-aged student at Upper Canada College, with a promising athletic record and the family interest in art. Two years of soldiering in England have matured him consider-ably and he now appears the battle-worthy young captain, khaki-clad legs stuck into muddy turned-down rubber boots, his battledress blouse encloses a spare figure; a lean lined head with a bristle of moustache emerges from the folds of a black turtle-necked sweater, and on his brow the Horse Guards badge shines like Betelgeuse. He is a happy com-panion with a great fund of anecdotes which he relates with the skill and timing of a practised raconteur.

We worked hard with "F for Freddy" troop. I recall a two-hour shoot at mid-day on the twentieth which, for very intensity, rivalled anything I had experienced. As was usual, I had my painting well advanced before the con-centration started, but these high muzzle velocity guns are most disconcerting. The snap of a twenty-five pounder, or the deep-throated bark of the medium, is relatively easy to absorb or, let me say one does acquire a dumb tolerance of such distractions while one works; they become, in this situation, the sort of occupational hazard for which one must cultivate a tolerance. But the 3.7 was in a class apart. The sense of penetrating shock which accompanies the firing of each round is something I should not wish to endure for more than two days. At the close of that two-hour barrage I doubted if I should ever hear normally again; the speech of my companions sounded vague and feeble, not unlike the strange auditory experiences one has on descending from a high altitude flight.

*   *   *

Main 40 was caught up in the mad intensity of the action. It was a restless, unpredictable location; unseen voices shouting above the normal din, vehicles mired, struggling men sloshing about in mud and water.

We had reached the winter solstice and by half past four in the afternoon of these monstrous days it was already getting dark and all the sinister apprehensions of the night were loose and at work, the quick startling illumination of muzzle flashes throwing the twisted framework of olive trees into fantastic relief, helmeted D.R.'s roaring breakneck through the mud, who knows where? Hughes emerged from the photo lorry with "Robby" Robinson behind him and we moved off together toward the mess tent for something hot. Bill Deery was in "E" mess, relating a maddening incident which had occurred during the fighting on our front: A group of Germans had suddenly broken cover and stood unarmed with their hands reaching for the sky. The Canadians were incredulous at first, but then they thought the Gerries may have been cut off, or perhaps had run out of ammunition. At any rate, they advanced to take them prisoners. They had not gone more than thirty yards when a withering flanking fire opened up on them from all sides and at the same time the decoy prisoners disappeared. Although our boys had gone to ground with the first long burst, casualties were heavy. Furious indignation seized the Canadians and, after unmercifully mortaring the enemy M.G. positions, they swept forward with heedless courage to revenge this unprincipled deception. As Deery put it: "It must have been mighty unhealthy for any paratrooper they caught up with."

A chill rain fell throughout the night to further hamper operations and added to the normal Martian sound-track were great shuddering detonations which we later learned came from Ortona. An oystery illumination announced another day, a day distinguished by the visit of two V.I.P.s. Among the limited divertissement afforded us on this bleak coast this was a most unusual event and we looked forward to it with curious interest.

Toward midday a cavalcade of cars lurched and bobbled into the area, preceded by M.P.'s and a score of anonymous War Correspondents. Out of a staff car, flying a C.I.C. pennant, stepped the Generals Montgomery and Eisenhower. Two more disparate officers, from the point of view of dress, it would be difficult to imagine: Monty the very soul of informality, cornflower blue eyes dancing above a casual and easy smile, on top his double-badged black beret, below the sheep-skin lined leather jacket, completely filling the popular ideal of 8th Army deshabille; Ike, on the other hand, equally affable, a model of sartorial perfection in the military sense, peaked forage cap, a beautifully cut American version of the British warm, riding breeches, and a pair of high shiny brown stove-pipe boots. There was no ceremony of receiving them; they simply left their vehicles in the visitors' car park and, accompanied by aides and members of their staff, walked down through our muddy tent lines in the direction of General Vokes' caravan. As they approached Hist. Sec., Hughes and I moved out toward the roadway to have a better look and as they passed we straightened up and saluted. At that moment Ike turned toward us and smilingly returned the compliment. When they had moved on Hughes pulled out his pipe, knocked out the ash on his hand and quietly observed, "Like all sycophants, I like paying a compliment to great men . . ."

Next day Main 40 moved forward. We had been operating out of that depressing mud-hole for eighteen days and I saw no sorrow or pain expressed as we turned north onto route 16, another rumour set aside; we were not bound for billets in Ortona. The liberation of that fateful town was resolving itself into one of the most difficult and bloody operations of the war. In San Vito Chietino ambulances were crowded around a municipal building which appeared to have been converted to use as an advanced dressing station and groups of bewildered refugees stood beside their meagre possessions.

A mile north of Marino di San Vito we turned into an orange grove of fantastic beauty, hung heavily with ripe fruit and knee-deep in gentle grasses which had kept it completely free of mud. These unexpected blessings were only very briefly enjoyed, however; an hour after our arrival they were just memories. After raising the camouflage net over our tent we started furiously to dig an "L" shaped slit trench. The R.A.F. were flying sorties that day and the Luftwaffe might well try a quick one while daylight lasted.

We were now within sight of Ortona and the stentorian voice of battle was harshly emphasized by this closer proximity. The southern approach to the town is flanked by numerous walled villas, in whose gardens stand stately palms and cypresses. These delimited areas, and the villas themselves, provided varied and formidable depth within which the defenders might fight. But this was no textbook battle, 17 pounders blasted unexpected holes in surprising places and hard-slugging merciless men from the west, wielding machettes, grenades, and bayonets, poured through upon the frantic defenders. Strong points were reduced one by one. Some paratroopers escaped, they were the lucky ones. The final gruesome killing ground was the Piazza Vittorio, a beautifully planted public square, fronting the town itself. Over these open gardens the hunted survivors, and the remnants of the rear guard, must withdraw at their peril. At last light scores of them lay among the fading asters and marigolds, grotesquely misshapen in death.

As night fell on that first evening at Marino, the Sitreps confirmed what we were all too conscious of, the clawing, tearing brutality of the fighting in the town. The Seaforths and the Edmontons were at the throats of the Paratroopers; it was a mediaeval battle in its close-quarter violence, groping through suffocating dust and smoke, stumbling over upturned furniture and debris, struggling breathlessly in nightmare

darkness, felling, clubbing, blasting, shooting it out. "They
are above us . . . They are in the next room . . . He is firing
from that upper window . . . Where is the Corporal? . . .
Hand me that Piat . . . Look out! It's booby-trapped . . .
Where? . . . You're sure? . . . Stand back! I'm going to let
them have it! . . . Flame jets rip through the splintering door.
The screams are lost as an earthquake blast rocks the neighbourhood. Tons of masonry, debris and household effects
rush into the street like grain from a hopper. The Jerry
sappers are systematically dynamiting buildings into the street
in a desperate delaying action. The barriers of rubble are
quickly sown with mines and covered by raking fire. Dust and
lead and fragmentation fill the flaming night.

The very smell of death and destruction reached us in
the orange grove, communicating its sanguinary message. A
holocaust of red glowed in the sky, revealing a ragged skyline
as tongues of flame leapt into the night. We peered through
the trembling darkness from a ring contour overlooking the
awesome scene. Down-wind from the action the frightful
intimate sounds of battle were all too clear, bursts of automatic
fire, the Bren and the Schmeisser answering one another,
each with its own distinguishing accent. A dozen concurrent
dialogues penetrated the blunter, duller, but more profound
thunder of the gunning. From the intervening vineyards rose
a ghostly vapour, like a shroud winding itself about the town.
The most boisterous and profane among us became silent
in face of what we witnessed. The morbid fascination of
destruction held us in its grip as life and its monuments dissolved before our eyes. Over all, the deafening voice of guns
beat a massive dirge like all the unmuffled drums of hell.

*   *   *

Thirty dreadful hours passed. Yesterday the town had
been hidden in the drizzle, a smoulderng unseen target,
battered and blasted incessantly by two armies. Not even the
soothing patter of rain on canvas had made rest possible.

On the one hand the phantasmal picture of the ghoulish fighting haunted us, on the other our mediums and field pieces
created hellish dissonance on the bench-land above, the enemy
responding with equal vigour.

Long before the grey illumination that was dawn came,
I wandered over to the mess tent in a fine drizzle. The early
morning lull was over and the gunners were at their mad work
again. Paul Boudreau sat in a corner alone, drinking coffee.
We were silent as the batteries behind us raged at the new
day. It was the morning before Christmas and no doubt Paul,
like myself, was reflecting on the tempestuous character of
this Christmas, compared with others we had known.

Frank Nutall, the Engineer L.O., breezed in whistling
"Begin the Beguine." "Say, you guys look as if you had seen
a ghost." Saying which he shouted "How about some mangaro,
Cookie?" Frank acted as if he had had a good night's sleep
somewhere, lots of bounce and good-natured evil in him. Frank
slipped the cook a couple of eggs and said "Uovo, turn 'em
over, lots of pepper." Slam went another salvo. "What do
those guys think they are doing with those pup-guns, Paul?"
"I wouldn't know, ask d'Arcy."

I moved toward the entrance as Mickey Burch came in.
Mickey was mess secretary and very concerned that we should
all pay our four hundred lire toward the NAAFI Cheer Fund.
The bottled stuff, like the mail, was expected some time today
and just would not be distributed to non-subscribers. The din
was growing outside and it looked as if day was never going
to dawn. I moved out into the gentle rain falling on the
greenest of green orange groves.

The batteries above us and in the Feltrino Valley behind
were relentless and fierce that morning and heavy counter-
battery fire was returning a violent answer. Sergeant Taylor
was already setting up his typewriter in the Hist. tent and
informed me that Hughes had gone back to A.D.M.S. to
recover his glasses, without which he is rather helpless. Our
orange grove had in two brief days assumed the appearance
of a floating island that has become dangerously water-logged.

A deep raw sienna mud reached half-way up rubber boots
and ever-widening lakes of surface water invaded the tent
lines.

*   *   *

Birmingham drove me back to "D" for Don Troop,
R.C.H.A. They were sited on the high plain between San
Vito and Appollinare. As we ground up the winding road
that leads out of the Feltrino, provosts halted us and warned
of a heavy stonk straddling the road just south of Appollinare.
I recognized one of my own boys from the "Volendam" and
we exchanged greetings. I thanked him for the warning, but
we were not going quite as far as Appollinare.

Harbouring the vehicle, I sloshed through mud to the
cave-like command post of Don Troop. The guns were slamming away viciously on all sides. They were deeply dug in,
the muzzle brakes just clearing the parapets and the gun
numbers almost wholly hidden from sight. I had learned
yesterday why this was so necessary on this unprotected
plateau. The whole area was torn and pitted with water-
filled shell craters and there were evidences of fresh spoil
which must have occurred during the night. They were
firing a steady barrage with the blue bags of "charge three"
littering the pits, accenting the prevailing gloom of the day.

Lieut. Marcel Sauve indicated a shelving corner where I
might sit. He had a big job on his hands and, in any case,
I had to wait for the shoot to end and the rain to cease. My
chill corner was filled with the dull bitter smell of powder
and shook with multiple concussions as "D" Troop raged
with impatient thunder at the unseen enemy. Capt. Rod
Philpot appeared, silhouetted in the entrance. He had been
most hospitable yesterday when I had undertaken a painting
of one of their sites, and now he welcomed me like an old
friend.

I returned to headquarters at mid-afternoon, wet, tired
and rained out. It had been impossible to do a thing. At the
Hist. Sec. tent, Hughes and Tucker-Burr were wrangling about

something, not an unfriendly argument, just a violent dis-
agreement about some aspect of civil life. But then, like the
day itself, every conversation was loud that afternoon.

*   *   *

We walked over in mortar-like mud and rain to the Men's
mess tent. The Sergeants and O.R.'s were already assembled
there and now we all stood together in the darkness, singing
carols. The sad throaty resonance of unaccompanied male
voices struggled with fitful success against the shattering noise
of battle raging all about us. A single candle wavered on
the table, faintly lighting the faces near it, seeming to symbolize by its frail light the innocence and gentleness of the
infant we praised. Otherwise one was conscious only of sound,
jagged, splintering sound, rending the night with violence.
Occasionally I could hear the voice of Trumbull Warren,
or of Richardson, or "Spike" Sprung, but, when it could be
separated from that other infernal din, our collective voice
was anonymous, a rich awkward nostalgic voice that seemed
an echo of the past, rather than the dreadful reality of the
moment. The reality was outside, we all knew that, but Christmas eve was a memory from another existence, a memory to
be cherished and recalled no matter what the circumstances.

The day had been one of concern for all of us. The enemy
had been reaching our Mediums effectively on the reverse
slope of the Feltrino with seventeen centimetre stuff and, at
the same time, burning up the Moro crossings. In the town
the battle of Ortona raged on with desperate fury. The Seaforths and the Edmontons were still embarked on the bloody
task of flushing the enemy from fortified houses in hand-to-
hand fighting which asked and gave no quarter. Tired,
drenched and mud-covered men blasted and tunnelled their
way from one house to the next like demon moles. The 48th
and the R.C.R.'s were out of contact, somewhere beyond the
lateral road, in their effort to circle the town to landward
and cut off the enemy's retreat to the north. Undoubtedly

Canadians were joined in the most bitter and costly fighting of the campaign on this Christmas eve. "Silent Night, Holy night . . ." we sang, reflecting uneasily on the mawkish anomaly of these familiar words. It was indeed the Holy night, wrenched and distorted with flame and dreadful sound, far from the peace and tranquillity that frames the story of Bethlehem.

Back through the chill darkness and mud to the tent lines, the ridge behind the H.Q. silhouetted by a flicker of muzzle-flashes. We were all quiet and reflective at this stage, in the midst of pandemonium, and the orange grove trembled with the shock of battle. Cottam joined us as we passed the "I" lorry and told of the desperate fighting even then proceeding in the Piazza San Francesco di Assisi, where the opposing forces, hidden in cellar and attic, were creating a deadly no-man's land of the cobbled square named for that gentle saint whose life had been dedicated to the simple ideals of brotherly love and self-denial. Cottam and the others waded over to the Hist. tent, a sad, dejected and forlorn company, among them Belmonte, Brown-Clayton, Douglas LaChance, Bill Deery, Hughes, Harris and myself. It taxed our small tent, but who minded on such a night. We discussed the nature of the battle. Textbook street fighting had been abandoned, had given way to the most desperately cunning and fanatically resourceful tactics. They were fighting with the technique of hard-rock miners. Dynamite, plastic explosives, stick grenades, piats. These were the drastic weapons which were so arduously and slowly reducing the town and the forces engaged. If such procedures were necessary to liberate every town on the peninsula, we were surely to spend many such dolorous Christmases together, if any survived.

The priority convoy from Bari had been only a rumour and we were without mail. The dreadful aching loneliness of that Christmas eve was never openly confessed, but it could hardly be concealed even by the hearty gaiety that generated so spontaneously in the Hist. tent that night. Eventually and inevitably we swung to talk of home. Belmonte produced

pictures of his son and daughter. His family lived at Forli,
just a very few miles away up this same east coast, a fact
which seemed to make his separation from them even harder
to contemplate. We talked of other Christmases and of the
story itself. Arguments ensued as different versions were
supported or challenged. Then Hughes rummaged in his kit
and produced a Bible and as Doug LaChance held a flashlight,
we read aloud from the second chapter of the gospel accord-
ing to St. Matthew.

Outside, in the rain-saturated darkness, the battle raged
with unflagging violence, heedless of the portents of the day
to come. One by one our companions left with a doubtful
expression on each face as they uttered the age-old greeting.
As Deery said "Merry Christmas" and disappeared behind
the tent flap, we heard a declining moan, like air escaping
from a child's balloon. We all looked at one another. Had
he been hit over the head with coshes? An enemy patrol
perhaps? An escaped prisoner? Swiftly these electrifying
thoughts crossed our minds as we rushed out, empty-handed,
to find him standing sheepishly, thigh-deep in muddy rain
water. He had fallen headlong into our water-filled slit trench.

*   *   *

It was still dark when a thundering blast awoke me. Our
own guns were relatively quiet, which added sinister emphasis
to the sharp percussion of enemy fire. These S.P.88's are
an uncomfortable menace and an unusual and unwelcome
intrusion on Christmas morning. I lay still, listening with
anxious alertness. The distant report of the gun could be
plainly heard, not a sharp report, but a rather hollow, ellip-
tical, whumpf! that had both time and tonality. The gun-sound
was followed in a second or two by an arched scream as
the eager shell cleaved the darkness and closed up on the
target. Then came the shattering KRUMP! as the missile
detonated. They appeared to be falling behind us and
markedly close, waking those recurring apprehensions about

the stray one, or the short one, or that misguided change of
angle that may pop one into your bedroll. As I rose, all
hell broke loose from our own guns, including the 7.2's
whose thundery voice might well "wake the dead." The
dawn was dark as the grave and chilly and the mud sucked
powerfully at my rubber boots as I wandered over in the
direction of "E" mess.

Above the man-made thunder I heard myself humming
the old traditional carol "God rest you merry, gentlemen,
let nothing you dismay." "Let nothing you dismay" seemed
to have a special significance this morning, a sort of mute
challenge to one's capacity for fortitude on a day which
brimmed with the make-ready for dismay. I saw our children
waiting impatiently in the hallway for the signal which would
start the family procession to the tree, the tree glistening
with tinsel and baubles and the tiny lights reflecting and re-
creating the surging legends of all past Christmases, the
enigmatic angel-face which peered from out of a dazzling
star like Aldebaran, filled with mystical significance, and
below, under the evergreen boughs lay all the gifts. This
nostalgic imagery rose in my mind and mingled obliquely
with a succession of deafening crashes as the 88's continued
to scatter their noisy greetings.

In the mess tent we tucked into an ample breakfast of
fried spam, powdered egg, and ersatz coffee. Everyone had
a "business as usual" attitude; little was said as each thought
over his own contribution to the violence that was to be done
that day.

The firing was heavy and continuous from both sides and
the savage gunning and blasting in Ortona could be distinctly
heard. The rapid tearing fire of the German machine pistols
and the somewhat slower chatter of the Brens, mingled
dolorously with heavier, blunter detonations to produce the
restless ragged cyclorama of violent sound, against which the
action proceeded. In the town the enemy produced a refined
sort of Christmas novelty in the form of a flame-throwing
tank. This bright new toy appeared briefly in the Piazza

Plebiscito, gouting savage squirts of flame like hot blood. But like Fafner, it was not invulnerable and gunners of the 30th Anti-Tank Battery plunged the sword *Nothung* into the monster's vitals and the unfortunate crews burned in the flaming furnace of their own fuel tanks.

Eric Harrison arrived as the drizzle set in again. We barely had time to greet him before walking over to the Advanced Air Support Tentacle. They had elaborate radio apparatus for relaying target information to air fields in the rear, and the operators had invited us to hear the broadcast of the King's Christmas Message.

Hughes and Harrison sat on a Sergeant's bedroll, I stood by the entrance, while everyone listened with thoughtful attention to the slow dignified measure of the King's sentences:

Once again from our home in England, the Queen and I send our Christmas greetings and good wishes to each one of you, all the world over. Some of you may hear me in your aircraft, on board your ships, or as you wait for battle in the jungles of the Pacific islands, or on the Italian peaks. Some of you may listen to me as you rest from your work, or as you lie sick or wounded in hospital. To many of you, my words will come as you sit in the quiet of your homes. But, wherever you may be, today of all days in the year, your thoughts will be in distant places and your hearts with those you love. I hope that my words, spoken to them and to you, may be the bond that joins us all in company for a few moments on this Christmas Day . . .

We realized full well that our families, no matter where, were listening at that moment to these gracious and thoughtful words. The Sovereign then went on to wish all who were on service "good luck and a stout heart." He sent messages of hope to our gallant allies, and thanked God for the generous strength of the United States of America and for the tremendous deeds of the Russians, and in conclusion said:

From this ancient and beloved festival that we are keeping, sacred as it is to home and all that home means, we can draw strength to face the future of a world riven by a tempest such as it has never yet endured. In the words of a Scottish writer of our day: "No experience can be too strange and no task too formidable, if a man can link it up with what he knows and loves."

We thanked the Air Tentacle boys and as I led Harrison
up a donkey path to the ridge beyond the headquarters, the
battle roared in ultimate fury and conversation was punctuated
by the jarring shock of gunfire. In civil life Harrison is an
associate professor of history at Queen's University, Kingston,
and an occasional visitor to Toronto. As we squished along
through the mud he recalled the unique cycle of circumstance
and locations in which I had provided accommodation for
him. On his last visit to Toronto before coming overseas he
had occupied my studio there. When he reached England I
had met him in Aldershot and given him the key to my flat
in Bayswater and now, on this Christmas night, near Ortona,
he was to occupy my pup tent at Divisional headquarters.
I warned that at last he was scraping the barrel of hospitality, as indeed he was to find out. The pup tent, consisting
of three Italian ground sheets buttoned together, provided
elementary shelter just one degree removed from sleeping
in the open. Eric specializes in English history, knows more
about Jasper Tudor and his despotic nephew Henry than anyone I have ever known, but his great pre-occupation on this
occasion was with establishing and equipping a Field Historical
Section, of which we would all become a part. Darkness was
settling on the orange grove as we returned from our walk,
the dim light of covered lanterns announcing the tent lines.

We heard the separate stories as the L.O.'s reported in.
Heavy fighting has been going on all day and is still going on.
Units of 1st Brigade who have been contacted and supplied
today claim they could easily have advanced and even breached
the Pescara road north of Ortona, but the difficulty would
have been to maintain supply lines. Transport in the field
is practically at a standstill. Our armour too is deeply mired
and, for all aggressive tactical purposes in open country, is
immobilized.

We had many visitors in the Hist. tent on this memorable
evening. Daood Raza, the L.O. from the Indian Division on
our left, was most charming. Like all young Indian officers,
he is very politically conscious, but these enthusiasms are

not unmixed with other interests in the arts and in literature.
He produced a letter from his sister in Lahore, written
in Pakistani, a delicate spidery hand, aesthetically beautiful
to look at, reminding one of some gentle form of fine needle-
work. When I enquired what the rather elaborate saluta-
tion meant, he said it was a very intimate and affectionate
form, addressing him as "My dear little chrysanthemum."
Captain Isolani, an Anglo-Italian idealist, had started off
with us as a prisoner interrogator, but since the Italian
armistice he had concerned himself with the more humane
problems of feeding the hungry, sheltering the homeless,
succouring the broken in spirit and body, and generally bringing what comfort he could to the daily columns of civilian
refugees who moved through our lines.

Our mess dinner was to be announced when it was ready,
but would not be before 1900 hours. Meanwhile the Hist.
tent bulged in the role of an ante-room as visitors continued
to crowd in. Kenneth Cottam and Ed. Kulbach roared with
laughter over some photographs they had found in a prisoner's
wallet. Eric Harrison pondered the quotation which had
concluded the King's message: "A Scottish writer of our
day . . ." "Probably Harry Lauder," someone volunteered.
"Who is he?" "Oh, don't you know? Sir Harry Lauder
wrote *Alice in Wonderland.*"

Norman Pope stuck his bonneted head through the tent
flap to receive a round of hearty-cum-abusive greeting. "So
this is where E mess has adjourned to. Runners are searching the clearing stations for you chaps." "Come right in,
Norman. Forget the runners and tell us how things go in
the town." A drink was put in his hand and a seat proffered.
"One of the roughest days they have had, but we think they
have had enough. Seems to be nothing but Paratroopers
left . . ." He then unfolded a remarkable story:

He had gone into Ortona to make a routine duty contact
with the Seaforths. It had been a particularly stimulating
journey from the brickyard in, with a picturesque fall of

nebelwerfers following his approach with alarming accuracy. At Battalion Headquarters, among other things, he had been told of the regimental Christmas dinner then proceeding in a parish church near the Piazza Vittoria. Since the whole town was a raging battleground of the most uncompromising close-quarter street fighting, he had been interested to know how it was being done. With some difficulty a guide had led him to the vestry door of the church and inside he had been confronted by a fantastic scene.

Over the crash and din of the surrounding battle came the skirl of bagpipes and the raised voices of men, singing Christmas carols. Through a smoky haze he saw men seated at tables covered with white napery. Three hundred yards away the enemy had active machine-gun posts, mortar bombs and shells of every calibre were creating a hellish dissonance, as cool young Subalterns served Canadian turkey with dressing, and vegetables to the men in the traditional way. An extra close shellburst would give rise to wild, defiant shouts and renewed energy lavished on the carols. All rifle companies were being relieved at their fighting posts, a platoon at a time, guided back to the church, fed this impressive meal, and then back to the line again. Besides turkey, the men had beer to drink, plum pudding, oranges, and nuts.

Everyone listened with silent intentness as Pope told the story. Unquestionably it was an inspiring Christmas story and through the minds of everyone must have passed the same proud thoughts. Rumour had it that the Edmontons were carrying out a similar ceremonial dinner in the very midst of battle, although the L.O.'s had not as yet heard the details. But the Seaforth story filled us with abounding hope and encouragement. With men such as these, come what may, we were bound to win through.

Mickey Burch appeared shouting "Come and get it!" and as the party slopped through the mud to E mess, Harrison said "I think I have it. It cannot be other than John Buchan, the Lord Tweedsmuir—"No experience can be too strange and no task too formidable, if a man can link it up with what he knows and loves."

*   *   *

As the battle roared to its climax, Harrison and I went for a long reconnaissance, walking up over the ridge behind the headquarters and along a donkey path through olive groves, pocked and scarred with shell holes and tank tracks. We came out on the high ridge above the Moro and looked across the plain toward Ortona. The town was being heavily shelled and several fires burned briskly near the sea. Through Harrison's glasses we could see that the south side of the town had suffered heavily. It lay like some fleshless skeleton, huddled shapelessly, half buried in rubble. Suddenly we saw the dome of San Tommaso dissolve in a cloud of dust and smoke. There seemed to be something symbolic about that destructive moment, as if the town itself had suddenly been felled and now lay senseless and prone, at the mercy of the battling forces.

Shellbursts were occurring all along the skyline ridge west of the town and in and around San Leonardo too. Out to sea the Adriatic was in a wild chop, as a chill east wind carried rain squalls toward us. We descended to the coastal road, through untouched groves of orange and nespoli, the hedgerows verdant, roses, asters and narcissus flowering in the gardens. Back at the section tent we found Matthew Halton and his charming colleague, Marcel Ouimet, interviewing Sam Hughes. It was, as always, a refreshing experience to meet and talk with intelligent visitors who could reconstruct events and points of view from the outside world.

Next morning we learned that Ortona had been cleared of the living enemy during the night. L.O.'s reported scenes of unparalleled horror in the northern sections of the town, where the enemy had been obliged to leave hurriedly without collecting their numerous dead. The mess tent was quiet, even sullen, that morning. It had been too long and costly a battle for us to experience much more than a profound sense of

PIAZZA SAN FRANCESCO DI ASSISI. WRECKED CHURCH OF SANTA MARIA DELLA GRAZIE, ORTONA.

BATTLE SCENE—(FANTASY)—VILLA GRANDE ROAD. ORTONA AREA.

relief; there was no consciousness of great achievement. True, the Division had added gloriously to its battle honours, but the piper had been paid a heavy price and now that it was over, all that seemed appropriate was to acknowledge the fact quietly.

Earlier on it had been hoped that the town and its valuable port facilities might be captured intact. So optimistic had we been about this possibility that a British balloon barrage unit had arrived at headquarters with balloons and gas tanks, all ready to float their equipment above the town and harbour. But they had vanished one rainy night and now, of course, there was no need for them. Even with the naked eye it could be seen that the enemy sappers had completed a very thorough job of demolition on the two great moles which extended out into the sea from below the town. No, Ortona would be of little value to us strategically; we had inherited little more than a useless pile of muddy rubble. But it was not this fact that was responsible for the depressive atmosphere in the mess that morning. It was the human loss that staggered everyone. We did not know the whole story at that time, but what we did know was sufficient for even the most hardened soldier to be saddened and reflective.

It was not a day when enthusiasms generated easily, but rumour, of course, always provides a basis for vicarious expression on the part of certain imaginative personalities around any headquarters. On this particular day, one of these creations insisted that with the capture of Ortona the Italian campaign was over and the initiative was now to pass to considerations of a western European invasion. This sounded reasonable, and evidence produced seemed convincing: The Generals, Montgomery and Eisenhower, had left the theatre to assume new commands; the 5th Canadian Armoured Division had done little for weeks and seemed likely to continue in that role. Some officers were even offering bets that a Canadian Corps would be formed, including 1st and 5th Divisions, and that we would be back in England by March, to begin training for our new role as the spearhead of a future western front . . .

*   *   *

Lawren Harris and I set out in the Humber for Ortona. Crossing the Moro bailey bridge, we wound up out of the valley, past Jasper Junction, the road lined with the sinister wreckage of war. Frequent Provost signs warned: "Is your journey necessary?", "Twelve rubbernecks were killed here yesterday," etc. At the crossroads we were stopped and questioned. The Provost seemed sceptical but accepted our explanation. From that point, into the town, we realized that this was the worst havoc we had yet seen. Screaming shells and nebelwerfers, with their dark trails of smoke, still fell among the ruins, destroying what had already been destroyed.

We parked the Humber in the Piazza Vittoria and picked a careful path along what had been the Corso Vittorio Emanuele. The familiar world disappeared, and in its place a grotesque and malignant forest of ruins crowded all about us, leaning, tottering crazily, reeking with the malodorous stench of death. We stumbled along in the tenebrous silence, incredulous of what we saw. Here indeed was the imagery of "purgatory" and the firm warning of the "instructor" seemed to guide us:

> Strict rein must in this place direct the eyes.
> A little swerving and the way is lost.

A gush of rubble filled the roadway, like a tumbling mountain moraine. Above it stood revealed, through tangled skeins of wire, the intimate furnishings of a tiny room, with pictures, washstand, and a tousled bed, dangling in upper space.

> Now the last flexure of our way we reach
> And to the right hand turning, other cares await us.

The Cathedral of San Tommaso stood half buried in its own masonry, looking as if a mighty cleaver had struck down through the dome and split it in half like a butchered steer.

The delicate baroque stucco and plaster work had dis-integrated under the blow and spewed into the piazza like so much blood and entrails. The great square campanile of the church still stood, shadowing the adjoining Palazzo di Pirris, but the face and high-collared cupola of the baroque super-structure was divided like the temple curtain, laying bare to the weather the delicate frescoed pendentives below the collar of the dome. The celebrated Portale, by Nicollo Mancino, had disappeared completely. Though fragments might be recovered, it could never again be the door through which the decorative courts of Alfonse of Aragon and Marguerite of Austria passed to worship, or to celebrate feast days, nor that Francesco Paolo Tosti remembered and loved. One wondered what had become of the ancient bas-relief that recalled the arrival of the boat from Illyria, bearing the precious casket containing the relic of the Disciple Thomas, or of a legendary early painted panel. Unless these were safely in the crypt it is doubtful if they still exist. Although Ortona had been sacked and burned on occasion during its violent past, the fabric of the church had always been respected and spared. But on this occasion an utterly ruthless and malicious enemy had reduced it in a deliberate and wanton act of destruction. In a hopeless effort to delay our pursuit the building had been mined and blown with demolition charges. It was said that we bulldozed a path through the crushed and broken masonry within fifteen minutes . . .

> Here the rocky precipice hurls forth redundant flames
> and from the ruin a blast up-blown, with forcible
> rebuff driveth them back, sequester'd from its bound.

The Via Monte Miella is a wide desolate thoroughfare imaginatively sited so that it commands a magnificent prospect of the snow-covered massif. Torn and muddied oleanders were strewn in its gutters and it was flanked by an abstraction of utter ruin. As we climbed over great hills of disintegrated plaster and masonry, we learned that a wall had just collapsed nearby, burying eight civilian workmen. What had been a school lay piled on our right, bleak window-less walls marking its outlines. At fifty yards I became aware of what looked like a picture, rising from the rubble. Closer inspection revealed it as a sepia photograph of the famous portrait of Michelangelo, usually ascribed to Jacopino del Conte. It had been pierced by fragmentation and moved feebly in the air, as if pleading for release, like some shock-ing item of super-realism. It no doubt had occupied a place of honour on a classroom wall, now the noble features of the great artist looked up at me from a scrabbled pile of brick and plaster. I moved aside the dusty stone, straightened out the picture, and put it carefully in my folio.

The Piazza Plebiscita presented another depressing rock pile, the Sherman tank "Amazing" tilted and brewed-up at its centre. We looked about in bewilderment and exhaustion. One felt a choking claustrophobia in the place. Everywhere was misery, death and destruction. I could not possibly paint, or even sketch, on that first dreadful visit. To think that a month ago this town had been intact, with most of its eight thousand inhabitants living here . . . A month ago the 1st Canadian Division had just left Campobasso, a vigorous, energetic, battleworthy force. How long ago it seemed since the convoys had climbed and fallen over the hills of Casacalenda and Larino, singing and wise-cracking, with supreme indifference for what the future might have in store for them. Pescara had then been the immediate objective and in the bursting enthusiasms of the moment it did indeed seem possible. On that approach march we knew little of what was in store for us, little of the terror that would strike us, little of the tearing and wounding, the mutilation and death. We were hurrying to overwhelm an enemy forced to abandon his chosen winter line and running for the next promising bit of cover. There might be rear-guard action, but he would not stop, he could not, if we pressed him hard enough. And Pescara did not look far on the map, forty-five miles at the most; a week, maybe ten days, should see us there. We had been filled with headlong optimism.

Then a disastrous factor had intervened: the weather had broken, and the rains had come. Though it might be thought that this factor should prove equally calamitous to the enemy, that was not the case. He was withdrawing over roads and bridges which were intact; he did not have to contend with unbridged rivers in flood, or the exasperating mud of the diversions. His supply and ammunition columns moved unimpeded in bad weather. In fact, rain and its accompaniment of low cloud, grounded allied aircraft and offered him the most favourable conditions possible for movement.

It has been suggested that if a pattern of dry, settled weather had held until December 10th, the battles of the Moro, and of Ortona, might never have assumed the magnitude and character that prevailed. It was the extraordinarily tenacious mud of the Abruzzi, and the flash floods that raged in every watercourse, that slowed the driving momentum of our attack. It would be wrong to assume that weather alone was responsible for the incidence and character of these battles. Everyone who took any part in, or witnessed the action, will agree that the German forces fought with fanatical stubbornness and desperation. But I think it must be agreed that weather and terrain offered them many advantages.

The important fact is that in spite of many physical disadvantages the 1st Canadian Division proved itself equal to the grim role it was cast in. Confronted with one of the toughest, bloodiest battles of the Italian campaign, this great Canadian formation earned a full share of glory in their valiant struggle, not only for the liberation of Ortona, but for that political and spiritual freedom which is the supreme ideal of western civilization and western culture.

Hiatus:

Toward the end of January nature smiled briefly and
benevolently. A few warm mellow days and the almond
and cherry trees burst into a profusion of blossoms; spirits
soared as the first premature indications of spring set the
sap rising in each individual blood stream. We left the
mildewed mess tent and ate our food in the open air, while
Hughes, the P.M.C., had the floor of the tent deepened a
further eighteen inches and lined with bricks. Similar imaginative projects, stirred into being by the persuasive sunshine,
were being undertaken all over the headquarters. And then,
just as suddenly as the warm spell had come, the weather
turned around, a wind rose, and it started to rain. The rain
changed to sleet and then to hail and, almost before we
realized it, we were back in the familiar environment of
tenacious mud. Just as quickly as the sap had risen, it fell,
and all was a wretched slough of despondency.

About this time there seemed to be much shuffling and
movement going on. Reinforcements were arriving and, with
them, new faces appeared. At the same time officers were
leaving the headquarters to resume regimental duty, or to
join that fabulous elite party who were returning to England
to undergo advanced training at Camberley. The rumour of
a Canadian Corps had long since been confirmed and had,
in fact, become a reality.

On the last day of the month, Sir Oliver Leese, the Army
Commander, appeared in company with General Crerar and
the next day we learned that we were under command of
1st Canadian Corps.

*   *   *

Rocca San Giovanni had been, until recently, an obscure
little walled town astride a ridge that pointed like an ageing
finger toward the sometimes blue waters of the Adriatic.
The front had swept over it in November, but good fortune,
or was it providence, had spared it the violence suffered by

neighbouring towns. It stood apart from the coastal road, like a thorn on a briar, proud, in a shabby sort of way, of its isolation, and indifferent to the endless military traffic that wound up out of the ravines that flanked the ridge.

Harrison had called me in from the Division for consultations and to consider the possibility of making paintings in and around the town while Corps was there. He and Jim Rowatt of the Edmontons were billeted in a tiny room above Renzetti's mercerie in the Battista Cesare. Renzetti's shop, at street level, served as the mess hall for a group of Corps officers.

With the arrival in the area of 1st Canadian Corps, Rocca had suddenly assumed a new dignity, having been selected as the location of Corps Headquarters. What the melancholy townspeople thought of this distinction was never revealed, although they occasionally spoke of happier days.

The misfortune of my stay in Rocca was that it occurred during a particularly wretched spell of weather in February. On my arrival, I looked out through the patched and broken glass doors of Harrison's room on still another weather-bound day. A north wind moaned through the curving tiles and a sleety-snow, "lumpy rain" as the Met. officer called it, swept down out of a dismal sky. The place was cold and damp, a condition hardly improved by the chill tile floors.

Plagued as we were at the time by most dismal weather, Rocca provided for me all the therapeutic wonders of a fashionable Spa. It combined the healing benefits of change, with a fresh set of rejuvenating associations that renewed my flagging spirit and freed me of a host of depressing tensions. Primarily we were away from the sounds of battle and somehow or other, regular sleep and the relative peace of the place brought with it a serenity of mind and a quiet composure I had not known for months.

Harrison carried out his duties in a little ten-by-ten room on the Corso Garibaldi, known as the "historical lavatory." This unsavoury title had grown up following the discovery

that a door in the wall, which obviously did not lead anywhere, when finally jimmied open, disclosed a tiny odoriferous
closet, barely a foot wide. Innocent of even the most elementary plumbing, it simply discharged its burden of corruption directly down the face of the exterior wall. With a
handkerchief to his nose, and an oath on his lips, Harrison
nailed the door shut again and tried to forget what it concealed. I made a sketch of him in this cold wretched little
room, with the sleet battering against the window.

Captain Ignatieff dropped in at one point with the first
so-called "sample" of gas-impregnated earth in a pickle bottle.
We all examined it intently although, for my part, I scarcely
knew what to look for.

Before Ignatieff left, Captain Taylor, the meteorologist,
appeared with a sheaf of retrospective weather reports.
"Don't ask me what the weather is going to be like tomorrow,
because I don't know," said he, sinking heavily into a chair.

*   *   *

They were a happy crowd at Corps, fresh in the situation,
but not devoid of a respectful appreciation of what was going
on in the forward areas. Many of them, as regimental officers,
had already seen battle service in this campaign.

I moved my painting equipment down to what was known
as the "Information Room." I was intrigued by this vaulted
cellar. It looked like some romantic movie director's idea
of what a front line military headquarters should look like.
Lit by two feeble electric light bulbs, which produced the
approximate effect of last light, and cast monstrous shadows
on the map-covered walls, it had the proper atmosphere too,
dark, draughty, and chill. Everyone sat huddled over their
paper work in greatcoats and mufflers, exchanging lively
banter with visitors about the sybaritic delights of the Italian
spring. Major Ian Wilson and Lieut. "Bill" Boss were among
the regular inmates of this dark dungeon. Visitors were paying calls every hour of the day and night from every forma-

tion in the Corps. As I worked away on a water-colour painting they never permitted a dull moment to mar any part of the time I spent there.

Fortunately every day at Rocca was not drenched in rain and occasionally the skies cleared and the increasing power of the sun gave us all hope. On one of these rare occasions we quickly organized a small expedition of those interested in making a reconnaisance toward the Basilica of San Giovanni in Venere.

*   *   *

We left the town by an ancient donkey path that descended into a deep ravine. There was a refreshing lift to the atmosphere on this particular day. The Maiella appeared very close, and even the distant Gran Sasso d'Italia, deep in enemy territory, hung in the sky like a painted stage drop, its jagged snow-covered peaks bathed in sunshine.

Crossing a stream, the path ascended the steep further bank between hedgerows, beneath which arum and hellebore grew among fragrant rosemary. Healey and Philip lead the way and behind me Harrison struggled in the mud. The farms on the plateau above were gay with drifts of fruit blossom and new lambs capered among the ewes.

Even at a distance we could hear the clangour of hammering and the ring of anvils, as if Vulcan himself was at work in the sanctuary of this consecrated ground. It turned out that a R.E.M.E. workshop was set up in the grounds surrounding the Basilica and the venerable romanesque building was surrounded by carriers and armoured fighting vehicles of all types, awaiting repair. How often in its long history had this weary masonry looked down on men in armour of a very different sort, their chargers bright with heraldry, champing nervously at the bit where now these carriers were harboured?

The great monument had a wild, disheveled "beat up" look about it, standing high on a ring contour overlooking the Adriatic and the wide estuary of the Sangro river, a

magnificent site which, unfortunately, had exposed it to
shell fire during the crossing operation in November. But in
spite of the intensity of that action it had not suffered exces-
sively. The walls and roof were holed in places, but the fact
that so conspicuous a building stood at all, lead us to believe
that it had not been a target.

It looked much like a great empty derelict hull, beached
and forgotten, as the Ark might have looked on Ararat.
Stripped of all former glory, its altars dismantled, its marbles
and mosaics vanished, the sacred vessels and missals of the
liturgy hidden, temporarily abandoned by its attendant monks
and clergy, it stood proudly, a noble monument, enduring
with impassive calm the indignity of modern war.

We moved round to the western entrance. The Basilica
had no arched portico or pronaos, it had no campanile, it was
just a great, unadorned, barn-like structure, the lower third
of the west facade was of travertine, the rest brick. Up a
short flight of stone steps, littered with shell fragmentation
and spent casings, a massive wooden doorway was approached,
on either side of which were deeply weathered, carved stone
reliefs. We could recognize the Virgin enthroned, and Daniel
in the lions' den, but the identity of an obscure gathering
of dignitaries eluded us. Healey suggested that it could
only be an Apochryphal "Orders Group." The style was
primitive and each episode was separated by antique acanthus
borders, which may well have come from the old Temple
of Venere.

The interior was empty and impressive, a simple romanesque nave of great dignity. At the eastern end was a flight
of steps, leading to an empty chancel, behind which was a
bare semi-circular apse. At either side, steps led down to
the crypt. More light than was normal entered through gaping
holes in the wall and roof, and debris from shell damage
still littered the floor. In the dark crypt were the fading
remnants of early frescoes, a baptism, a Madonna and
Child enthroned, with possibly St. Michael and St. Nicholas
of Bari. We were told that these frescoes had been painted

in the late twelfth century by Luca di Pallustro da Lanciano.

In the cloister garden two large dun-coloured mess tents had been raised, and personnel of the R.E.M.E. unit appeared to be billeted in cells that led off the cloister. It was here that we saw the fragments of the early Roman temple of considerable archaeological interest.

The hammering and welding continued in the wide space surrounding the church, and the blue smoke from coke fires hung in gauzy veils around the soldier tradesmen.

*   *   *

Early in January it became evident that at least a temporary lull in the fighting had been reached, and the line began to stabilize just north of Ortona. This did not mean that action ceased. Constant patrolling, alternating with sudden fierce set-piece encounters, kept us alive to the fact that the conflict still went on, and the artillery of both sides hammered away at selected targets, taken on at the most unexpected and inconvenient times.

During this period, I painted a number of subjects, relevant to the December battles, which had been difficult to tackle while the fighting raged at its full intensity. Such locations as the Casa Berardi, the Berardi crossroads, San Leonardo, and Roatti, provided material of historic interest, and I developed many paintings in Ortona itself.

It was while I was in Ortona one dark day in mid-January that I saw two red hats come bobbing down the Corso. As they disentangled themselves from the other khaki-clad figures on that battlescarred thoroughfare, I was surprised and delighted to discover that one of them was Colonel J. A. MacFarlane, Dean of Medicine at Toronto. After warm greetings and some leading personal questions, the conversation centred around how and where he might see some of my paintings during his brief visit to the Division. I readily accepted his invitation to dine in San Vito that evening and bring what was available with me.

We met in 2nd Field Dressing Station, crossed the street to a smoke-filled saloto for an aperatif, then walked over to the new officers' club. "The Sword and Drum" provided a noisy repetition of what one had experienced many times before, strenuous vocalists above a wheezy Italian orchestra, heard through a drumfire of laughter and conversation. The food was army rations disguised in minor ways and aided by rooster blood vermouth. Through it all, we sat reminiscing with Lieut-Col. Boyd of Otawa, officer commanding the 4th Field Ambulance, and after dinner I accompanied him back to the 4th so that I might visit Ed. Kulbach. In the next bed was Marcel Ouimet, the war correspondent, a very impatient young man. I tried feebly to console them both.

Back at the 2nd Field Dressing Station, I was astounded to find that an operating room had been decided upon as a suitable place for the exhibition of my paintings. A converted school room, reeking with the pungent fumes of heady antiseptics, and centred by an arclight that beamed a powerful vertical ray onto a gleaming white operating table, provided a unique atmosphere for the purposes of an art exhibition, but then the paintings themselves had been conceived and executed under rather abnormal conditions, and since the viewers were medical men, possibly the incongruity of the situation might not strike them as forcibly as it did me. I placed the first painting against a pillow, directly under the light, and turned to face the fifteen doctors who stood close round the table, some in white, some in khaki, a most enthusiastic audience.

*   *   *

The great massifs of the Appenines were deep in snow; the Maiella, immediately to the west of our positions exposed unbroken contours of purest white. The weather had been consistently bad, sleet and hail alternating with driving snow flurries. The area of the Indian Division, high up on our left, was snowbound, and we understood that their men were suffering considerably from the cold. The bivies, tents, and lorries of Main 40 had been set up in a sea of mud, shank-deep, and of the most extraordinary plasticity. On those rare days when the sky was clear, the air had an eager nip and nights were cold, half an inch of ice on the water buckets each morning.

The routine of an Army war artist, during this winter campaign, started at first light. After performing his ablutions quickly, he made directly for the relative warmth of the mess tent, where he usually learned what had transpired during the night and what was likely to happen during the day. If an impending action appeared to take precedence over his planned activity, he would talk it over with the historical officer, come to some decision, and then arrange transportation.

On this particular morning, Lawren Harris and I were on our way before eight o'clock. We followed the coast road, across the Moro Bridge, wound up out of the ravine, past the church of San Donato, where the Canadian cemetery was to be, crossed the triple-double, and finally reached a point on the Orsogna-Ortona lateral where the sideroad leads off to Villa Grande. Having found a location, Fiddler harboured the fifteen hundred-weight, and we commenced our reconnaissance.

In a peacetime situation this is the critical initial phase that precedes the making of a field sketch. The perceptive faculties turn over the possibilities latent in the complex forms that present themselves, discarding them or resolving them into patterns of thought which may result in a composition. On a battlefield, recently fought over, a preliminary reconnaissance includes all of these considerations, but in addition one must also be alert for the cleverly concealed mines and traps, left lying about to catch just such unwary people as war artists. One may trip over a wire, open a door, pick up an attractive looking something, and do so for the last time, as I had witnessed in the past. Our reconnaissance, therefore, was a careful one.

Each of us found a location, searched the area for deviltries, and then for a slit trench or shell-hole, just in case.

Firing was sporadic and uneven that morning. Although we could hear the stuff whistling through the air above, it was not falling anywhere near us. Having settled on a location, I then returned to the 15 cwt. to get a three-ply board out of my khaki canvas folio and attach a fresh sheet of water-colour paper to it. The fundamental idea behind the selection of equipment for painting in the field was that it must be possible for the artist to handle it himself, unaided. Water-colour equipment was therefore the answer. I had stand-ardized the size of each individual painting to approximately 15″ x 21″, or half a sheet of standard water-colour paper. I carried a collapsible field sketching easel and a small metal stool. I shouldered this paraphernalia, returned to my location, and was soon immersed in the problems of my subject.

One of the risks of our work was that one became deeply preoccupied, and danger was upon one before it was realized. Danger could disclose itself in many ways. Sometimes a noisy ricochet would alert one to the fact that artillery targets were shifting, or a sudden, unpleasantly close burst might distract one momentarily. The air was continually alive with our own craft, but occasionally ME's or FW's dived from the clouds, surrounded by ack-ack bursts and tracer. Down they would come, with those funny little black crosses on their wings, and then came the bombs. Depending on how close they were, we made notes on the spectacle for future reference, or we got into the cover we had previously recced. Our days were never dull, never without interest, never without excitement. What we painted under these conditions was never what we might have done in the contemplative quiet of a studio, but we were getting the raw material, the eye-witness experience, which should lend authority to any-thing we might eventually do in relation to the campaign.

At lunch time, we left our easels where they were, and moved back to the truck, where Fiddler already had the tea made and was heating "M and V" over an improvised fire. The general practice in Italy, for producing a small bivouac

fire was to take an empty tin can of suitable size, and per-
forate the upper half only. The lower half was then filled
with a clod of earth, which was soaked with gasoline. When
the earth was lighted it produced a hot blue flame that would
boil a kettle in short order. Unfortunately, it was not the
sort of heat that warmed the soldier too, and invariably we sat
around, blue and cold, supping "M and V" out of a mess tin.

Having eaten a meal, we returned to our painting which
we pursued to its completion, or until the declining January
light, reduced even further by overcast skies, made further
work impossible. Dismantling our equipment, we then returned
to the 15 cwt. and drove back to Headquarters.

These winter experiences were uniformly miserable. The
Abruzzi coastal plain has a penetratingly damp chill climate,
a fact which could in no better way be appreciated than by
sitting out all day on a sketching stool. Added to this were
all the elements of risk, latent in a theatre-of-war situation.
On many occasions we were obliged to spend precious daylight hours in cover. On one such occasion Harris and I
were engrossed in a project near Casa Barardi when we heard
the ominous roar of tank engines. Presently we saw two
Shermans, harbouring in a nearby farm yard. Barely five
minutes had passed before a series of black ranging bursts
cracked in the air above us. Then came the real thing and our
day was ruined.

Our journeys to and from location were often anxious
ones. The Gerries liked to lay down occasional stonks on the
line of roadways and they had them very accurately ranged.
We were often preceded and followed by multiple shell bursts
which straddled the road and crashed in the ditches. Of
course, everyone in the situation was subject to the same
treatment, but there were many occasions on which we felt
ourselves very fortunate to get back to Headquarters with
a whole skin.

*   *   *

Toward the end of our stay on the Ortona front in
March, the two Colonels commanding the Historical Section

arrived at Headquarters in San Vito to inspect the personnel
and functioning of the Field sub-units. Mid-month the weather
had improved considerably. The floods receded and the mud
began to dry out. We prayed for rain so that they might
share the misery that had been our lot throughout the winter,
but alas, our prayers went unanswered until the day before
their arrival when heavy showers gave promise of ideal conditions for the reception. As we returned to rubber boots and
trench coats, one member of the Section was heard to say
"The Lord has delivered them into our hands." Unfortunately, the Lord did nothing of the kind. They came and
went in cool but agreeable weather.

Colonel Fortescue-Duguid had been a gunner with the
2nd Field Regiment during the First World War and was
now the Director of the Historical Section in Ottawa. Colonel
C. P. Stacey directed the overseas operations of the Section
from C.M.H.Q. in London. They were both exposed to heavy
schedules of conferences and excursions during their visit,
which is always the case on such occasions. Harrison and
Hughes did most of the conducting, but on one occasion I
had the privilege of escorting Colonel Duguid back to the
2nd Field Regiment and the actual battery he had served
with in 1915, an event which gave him much pleasure.

Following the Colonels' departure, it was obvious that
the Ortona front was being prepared for a holding action
only, and that it was not to be us who were to hold it.
Miles of concertina wire were being erected, something I had
never seen employed in the area before. There were rumours
of movement and every indication of impending new de-
velopments. General Crerar had left Corps early in March
and been replaced by General Burns. On the 7th we had
returned to the command of the 5th British Corps. A new
excitement and fresh speculation animated "E" mess as the
mild April sunshine encouraged us to have our meals in the
open once more.

At breakfast one morning conversation was just blooming, under the stimulation of what passed for coffee, when

the Divisional defence. Bofors and Brownings went into heavy action. Over the Headquarters came a low-flying Spitfire, rolling and plunging to clear the flak and make recognition possible. He was surrounded by black ack-ack bursts and streaks of tracer. Then we saw what the real target was, an M.E.210 returning, no doubt, from bombing the Sangro crossing. Dark smoke streamed from his fusilage and he was losing altitude rapidly. He disappeared behind the trees and crashed on the north side of the Moro valley. Later, I examined this plane. It was still smouldering and smelt strongly of carbide. The most interesting thing about the wreck was that the black-edged white cross had written at its centre in pencil the first two lines of La Marseillaise, "Allons enfants de la patrie, le jour de gloire est arrivée . . ." There was no possibility of this inscription having been written in following the crash because the pencilling was smoked over. We concluded that the machine had either been assembled or manufactured in France and that a patriotic workman had inscribed it at that time, or that it had been in transit through France where possibly some youth had found satisfaction in such daring. We dismissed the idea that it had been done by the Maquis. Had any member of that organization approached closely enough to write on enemy aircraft, a much more violent act would have been committed. However, there it was. Someone had written these rousing lines at considerable risk and it was a stirring experience to discover them.

*　　　*　　　*

Main Headquarters of the 1st Canadian Infantry Division had been located in the orange grove near Marino di San Vito four months to the day when we moved out and started on a series of journeys that would take us to the savage battles around Cassino and in the Liri valley. In a quiet drizzle of rain, the column moved off one morning in late April and we looked on Marino for the last time. The reverse slope of the Feltrino was freshly green and beautiful. The fig trees spread yellow fan-like shoots, fruit blossoms were tightly packed along the boughs, looking almost artificial in their abundant whiteness. The valley was lush with new vegetation and life. Marino, a location filled with horror and beauty that none of us would or could ever forget, was gone.

In three bounds we were back in Vinchiaturo, where the Camp Commandant, Major Clemis, waved us on to a location just off the Gildone Road. We pitched our tent on a rising slope overlooking the Matese massif and the valley of the Biferno, one of the most impressive camp sites we had had. As I listened to a cuckoo, calling in the dark woods before me, I reflected on the welcome contrast that vivid pastoral experience provided to the shriek of shells.

That morning we had left a staging camp at Larino, a small town gay with clematis and purple lilac, built around a Roman amphitheatre. Climbing through solemn treeless foothills, we sighted the citadel of Campobasso soon after passing Matrice. It was nearly five dreadful months since that gay, devil-may-care Canadian force had left Campobasso, following this very same road. I looked in reflective silence as Ferrezzano appeared on its conical hill and other familiar features of the location asserted themselves. Do not mistake me, we were still a blithe and daring force, but our composition had changed considerably. Many of our reinforcements were seeing Campobasso for the first time.

One of the interesting facts of this journey was that at Larino we were ordered to remove all identifying marks, tactical signs, unit badges and patches from uniforms and vehicles. We were to pass through Campobasso incognito; the Command was anxious to make our movement as secret as possible. We could all appreciate the significance of this order, it was not desirable that enemy agents should realize that the Canadians had been withdrawn from the Adriatic.

It will be recalled that Campobasso had been liberated by the Canadians in October, 1943, and that during the October-

November period of that year it had been a Canadian rest centre, re-named "Maple Leaf City." During that memorable period many friendships had been established between us and the townspeople, friendships that could not readily be put aside. In addition, the Canadians as a collective group had been liked for their frank directness and honesty, and for their generosity which had been expressed in many ways.

The convoy descended the hill, passed under the great buttress of rock on which the Castello Monforte stands, and entered the town. Almost immediately cries of "Il Canadese!", "Buon Canadese!" rose from the populace and spread like wildfire through the streets. They waved from sidewalks, balconies and windows. It was like a triumphal homecoming. For a while we remained silent, but obviously the cat was out of the bag and very soon we did the only thing that was possible, we waved and shouted back.

*   *   *

The barrage, which heralded the opening of the campaign in the valley of the Liri River, began at 2300 hours on 11th May, so that the Canadians had very little time between their withdrawal from the Adriatic front and their costly participation in that desperate sequence of battles.

The 1st Canadian Infantry Division was now considered to be once more "At rest," but actually we were engaged in vast preparations for our new rôle, reorganizing, re-inforcing, re-equipping, training. Two days following our arrival in Vinchiaturo, I received a signal from Harrison, directing me to appear at Corps, then located at Raviscannina. On arrival there I found that he wanted me to do some portraits of newly decorated other ranks, and paintings of back echelon activities at Avellino, all before the Liri campaign started.

I found the region a most attractive place. It lies on the warm southern slopes of the Matese, at the foot of which flows the great Volturno River, with Capua possibly twenty-five miles away. Characteristically, 1st Canadian Corps was under canvas in an olive grove which had been a mud-hole earlier but fortunately was now bone-dry. The area is surrounded by heavily wooded foothills and dominated by the ancient Castle of Sant Angelo.

I had spent Easter at Corps in early April, during which time Harrison and I had climbed the nearby hill to examine the castle. As we walked through the village on our way up, we encountered the local Good Friday procession emerging from the church. A dark villager led the procession, bearing a huge black cross. Behind him followed a mixed group of singing children with thin reedy voices. Pallbearers carried a life-size prone figure of the multilated body of Christ, morbidly realistic. Behind the effigy marched a solemn group of elders in white gowns with scarlet capes and hoods. Then came a life-size figure of the Virgin, fully clothed and crowned, carried high on the shoulders of strong men. Then a motley, tuneless, leaderless band and, bringing up the rear, the women of the village, walking slowly and chanting some unfamiliar litany. It was a strange, almost mediaeval sight, the weird harsh flat music, the thump of the drum, the untrained voices, the cluttered step of the marchers, but most significant of all, the devoted interest of the participants. I have forgotten many of the organized processions I have seen, but this one I shall never forget. They walked around the village and then up a Via Dolorosa, past the stations of the cross, to a pink chapel on the hillside which contained the calvary.

We continued our steep walk up a hedge-crowded lane. Beneath the hedges grew alternate brilliant clumps of wild cyclamen and anemones. Emerging onto an open boulder-filled pasture, the last steep grassy climb to the tumbled walls was strewn with daisies, among which lay hundreds of S.S.A. spent casings and rusting shell fragments. The Americans had advanced up this valley in December.

The castle was a magnificent ruin of obvious Norman origin, commanding a stupendous view of the valley from its isolated hilltop, possibly six hundred feet above the shining

surface of the river. There was no moat or ditch around
it, but the plan of the outer curtain wall, what had been the
towered gate, the bailey, and the inner keep, were all discernible. The apse of a tiny chapel still held fragments of
an ancient fresco. Looking down from this commanding
height we could see the village of Sant Angelo, almost hidden
on the vine-clad hillside below, and from that direction the
melancholy music of another village procession reached us.

After supper that evening, I went to Harrison's tent where
a small gathering of friends, Bob Pilot, Jack Vaughan, and
John Bassett, sat eating walnuts, drinking marsala, and discussing the differences in character between St. Francis and
St. Dominic.

                    *   *   *

Having completed the portraits, I then moved on to the
2nd Echelon formations at Avellino. Summer seemed suddenly
to have descended on us with satanic violence and the old
environment of mud was now replaced with choking, blinding
dust. On the long reach of the road through Pietroviaranno,
visibility was at times reduced to forty yards.

We reached Naples around lunchtime, climbed the winding Via Rosa to the Vomero and then drove over to the
Allied Officers' Club in Possillipo. We lunched on a balcony
overlooking the glories of the bay. But Vesuvius, who had
erupted in early March, was a dormant static mountain, the
normal plume of smoke absent, and the southwest slope of
the cone dusted grey with lapilli.

On reaching the open country again, after leaving Naples,
the lovely black-top highway was lined with flowering trees
and shrubbery, azalea, oleander, clematis, pink and white
horse-chestnuts, and fruit blossoms in great abundance. We
reached the hills at Montesarchio and then that long tunnel
of ilex trees led us into Avellino.

At the Villa Barra I presented myself to the hospitable
Colonel "Mike" Dunn who left no stone unturned to see that
I was comfortably accommodated, and that I received full

co-operation in carrying out my programme of painting. In peace time, Avellino is an attractive little town nestling in a well-wooded valley, beneath the towering peak of Monte-vergine, but in war time it was dusty and unkempt. The principal square, the Piazza Garibaldi, was plastered with Communist signs and legends: "Ogni cosa e'sudor nostri ercoli," "Viva l'armata rossa," "Lavoretori unitivi," "Viva Stalin!" These were crudely painted in black and red lettering on the walls of buildings.

My paintings of the "Postal tracing section" and of that vast sea of faces in the "Part Two Orders Office" went well and after Harrison joined me I found time to move about. Brigadier E. W. "Eric" Haldenby, Officer Commanding the Headquarters of No. 1 Canadian Base Reinforcement Group, and an old friend and neighbour, recommended that we visit the Santuario at the top of Montevergine. He also told us of the treasure from the National Museum in Naples, hidden in the monastery at Loreto. We lost no time in investigating both of these leads because time was running out. The hiatus that had begun with the liberation of Ortona was drawing to a close.

*   *   *

From behind a closed door, the familiar measures of a Bach fugue reached us as we waited, the unseen pianist playing with an easy grace, repeating certain passages as if enjoying their cadence. We listened with relaxed interest until footsteps announced the approach of the *Superiore*.

He was an older man, attired in the same white habit, and wearing a tonsore, a thin line shaved to the pate, circling his head like a halo. He greeted us most cordially and, after making a number of polite personal inquiries, invited us to view the treasure.

A younger man led us upstairs to the floor above. The Monastery is a characteristic baroque building, designed by Antonio Vacaro, and built about 1730. We had entered a wide corridor whose windows overlooked a central quad-

rangle or courtyard. The young Brother pointed out that
before the war, it had been a luxuriant garden, today it
supported a very substantial crop of potatoes. The corridor
had the appearance of a storage warehouse. No attempt
had been made to conceal its precious burden of crates and
packing cases, containing pictures, books, manuscripts, and
other treasure. In view of the barbarous destruction inflicted
on the Neapolitan archives, by the enemy, it was consoling
to realize that at least the contents of these cases had been
saved for posterity.

Yesterday we had visited the Benedictine *Santuario* on
the summit of Montevergine. Having heard of a fabulous
Byzantine painting of the Virgin there, we had climbed the
thirteen mile mountain road to that celebrated shrine, three
thousand feet above the town.

The church, in which the painting reposes, is in good
baroque style. I was unable to learn either the name of the
architect, or the date of its building, but it appeared to be
early eighteenth century.

The Madonna of Monte Vergine hung in a side chapel
in a tenebrous atmosphere of mysterious dark beauty. We
viewed the sacred image through wrought metal gates, which
precluded any critical examination of its surface, but she
looked straight at us, solemnly and enigmatically, with a calm
almost hypnotic gaze. The painting was dark, as was the
chapel, and the silver-gilt adornments seemed jewelled, as
they reflected the wavering light of many candles.

As I met the intent gaze, I found something uncommon
in this work which I had not associated with icon painting
before. It seemed to lack the elegance and delicacy, characteristic of the Constantinople School. Possibly it was its size.
It seemed overdramatized and the superimposed adornments
just a little excessive. What I felt was not disappointment,
but rather surprise. The Brother, who was with us, said that
he had heard that only the head itself had originally come
from Constantinople, and that the rest of the figure had been
added much later. This might well have been the case and

might account for the fact that the painting is seldom
referred to as a great work of Byzantine art. But it is powerfully attractive and it has claimed the most wide-spread devotion from supplicants in this region. At Whitsuntide, and
on the occasion of the Nativity of the Virgin in September,
there are massed pilgrimages to this shrine and Neapolitans
climb the mountain on foot to prostrate themselves before this
sacred image of *Mamma Schiavona.*

It was while viewing this celebrated painting that the
Benedictine Brother mentioned the treasure stored at the
foot of the mountain in the monastery at Loreto. He must
have appraised us as wholly trustworthy individuals, because
he confided that a great number of paintings from the National
Museum in Naples had been hidden there. Recalling my
pre-war visits to that great institution and having in mind
Brigadier Haldenby's suggestion, I resolved to pay a visit
to Loreto.

We moved along the corridor, avoiding the packing cases
with some difficulty, and entered a dining-hall or refectory.
A continuous table ran around three sides of this hall, laid
with spotless white, indicating that a meal was about to be
served. Before each place was a piece of bread and an oval
white plate, on which rested a simple carafe, filled with an
amber-coloured wine. The rich aroma of Italian food per-
meated the hall, inspiring a sympathetic gurgle from somewhere under my bush shirt. However, our invitation had not
included lunch and, in any case, my interest had been deflected
immediately to the walls.

There, to my astonishment, I saw what my eyes could
hardly credit, that great series of Flemish tapestries, designed
by Bernard van Orley, which in peace time hang in the *Salone
degli Arazzi* at Naples. Having proven too large to hang
separately, they hung overlapped in heavy golden layers,
jostling one another for breathing space.

These tapestries represent grandiose episodes of that
sanguinary battle, fought outside the walls of Pavia, between
the forces of His Imperial and Catholic Majesty, the Emperor

Charles V and those of his no less exalted rival, the unfortunate Francois I, King of France. One peers through the costly magnificence of them into the clamorous violence of a sixteenth century battle. Hirsute landschnecht wield dagger and blade against Swiss yeomen, Spanish arquebussier fire and reload their ponderous muskets, protected by a great press of desperate halberdiers, parrying and thrusting at a wild, shouting tangle of pikemen. The mounted chivalry, in plumes and gilt-edged armour, strike pompous attitudes under waving banners. While apparently urging on their troops in the heat of battle, they observe a nice regard for seat and hands, and the proper wear of accoutrement. One is staggered by the wealth of detail, the vast, struggling, Cecil B. deMille crowds of costumed soldiery, the forests of lances that sway across the backgrounds, lending extraordinary realism to these moving battle scenes. Except for the same necessity to destroy the enemy, there is little relationship to modern battle. Even where forces equal to those at Pavia are engaged, the modern battlefield would appear empty of men. Today, we seek tactical advantage from cover, concealment is the device employed in manoeuvring. Darkness, camouflage, dispersal, smoke, deception, surprise, anything, to hide the real intention until the *coup de grace* is delivered. A different problem is posed for the war artist today than that so magnificently faced by Van Orley.

At Pavia, the forces were drawn up in battle array on that cold February morning, in full view of one another, and not until the trumpets sounded did the screen of pikemen advance, protecting the musketeers, and after that first volley, the ordered array was transformed into the picturesque brutality of close hand-to-hand encounter. Great sturdy landschnecht, with hefty butts and calves and decorated cod-pieces, straddling their prostrate comrades, dealing out limb-severing, skull-crushing, mutilation on the enemy.

They are a ruthless, merciless sequence, if viewed piecemeal in descriptive detail. Yet all their bloody havoc is

transmuted and resolved into the elegant, decorative term-
inology of Cinquecento art, through Van Orley's magnificent
orchestration and the remarkable skill of the Flemish weavers.
One is only conscious of sumptuous regal splendours, as were
agreeable in a gift to the puissant majesty of the Emperor
Charles V.

The warm, spicy smells of Italian victuals were distract-
ing. Both Harrison and I felt fortunate to have had a glimpse
of these treasures in their war-time hideout, but the Brother
seemed anxious that we move along. No doubt the meal was
on the point of being served. We left the refectory and continued down the corridor, recording a catalogue of intriguing
names and an impression of golden beauty.

The Liri Valley:

Visibility was a truck-length and we had difficulty keeping
the vehicle ahead of us in view. The pitted track was hub-
deep in yellow dust, which billowed up around us in blinding
clouds. Above, a pitiless sun blazed down with the oppressive
red heat of noon. Occasionally an errant gust of air swept
aside the sultry curtain, revealing the green beauty surrounding us.

Club Route struck across undulating fields of red poppies
and deep blue lupins, without reference to any previously
existing roadway. The waving wild flowers existed in such lush
profusion as to fairly paint the landscape. I languished in
partial suffocation as we high-balled along in the dusty heat.
The jeep swerved around a bomb crater and we seemed
to have lost the precious white tape, our only guide except
for the vehicle ahead which, more often than not, was lost
in the dust curtain.

Heavy accumulations of signal wire lined the hedgerows;
defused box and teller mines were exposed and scattered
everywhere. We were impressed with the accuracy of the

air bombing; many of the craters were fifteen feet wide and ten deep, patterned both on and beside the track and rimmed by mountains of spoil. The convoy slowed up, we closed on the three-tonner ahead of us, the dust blew off to the left and the green world reappeared.

Monte Cassino rose boldly on our right, flecked with cloud shadow and dazzling sunlight. The ruined Benedictine Abbey lay grey on the summit, eroded and worn away with blast and fire, a lamentable sight. Here was one of the oldest seats of learning in Christendom, where the lamp had burned through the darkest ages. Had it been extinguished in this enlightened twentieth century? What of its library, its refectory? The Alati cloister, the vault of the church, decorated by Luca Giordano, the chapels by Francesco de Mura and Solimena? It was an unhappy theme to reflect on. Although we had heard no detailed information concerning the extent of the destruction, there appeared to be no doubt but that the great monument had been deeply ploughed.

On the move again, the scene, like our reflections, was consumed in dust. The three-tonner had turned off on a side track and we were now following another jeep. As we closed on it, I noted a familiar black beret and a pipe jutting from a dusty head. By good fortune we had overtaken Sam Hughes, bound, no doubt as we were, for the Headquarters of the 1st Canadian Division.

The Liri River appeared occasionally on our left as the dust permitted and we seemed to be following a road that paralleled its course. The country was close, not unlike parts of England. Heavy hedgerows enclosed fields of grain and hay and the forestry was deciduous woods of elm, birch, and oak. The roar of mortar and artillery fire grew louder and the sky was ominously filled with aircraft.

*   *   *

Main 40 was a busy, tense place. Personnel carried on bright-eyed and wary; mortar bombs and shells searched the area with persistent and thorough interest. Lorries and bivies were craftily harboured and camouflaged, but to what purpose? The enemy quite evidently knew where we were.

However, we needed no incentive to start digging immediately. The situation was self-evident: we were back once more, inside the storm centre of battle. Hughes had shocking news, Major George Renison, G.S.O.II, had been seriously wounded on the 15th and Lieut. Dicky, the G.O.C.'s aide, had been killed. This and other reports did not add to our composure.

Having completed reasonable shelter in the camp area, we set off to recce the terrain ahead of us. Emerging from scrub woods onto a knoll, we were told that a ragged line of poplars a mile away marked the forward areas of the Adolf Hitler Line. To the left was the battered, ruined, burning town of Pontecorvo. Except for flights of aircraft, and their normal background of flak above us, not a moving thing was to be seen on the ground. Shelling was continuous and the witches' shriek of incoming nebelwerfers slashed the sunny sky with creeping smoke trails.

Our companions pointed out the direction of the target area and we watched the sky expectantly. A large force of panzers had been observed, deploying on our left flank, and an order had gone back to air support to engage this concentration. Nothing could be seen of the tanks at this moment, but their location was soon very apparent as, with a mighty roar, our aircraft appeared out of the hot sun. The first wave dived steeply and bombed. Great blue-black beacons of smoke mushroomed near the town. The second must have caught the target dispersing. In addition to bombing, they returned again and again to strafe the area heavily. As each plane blew its final kiss and turned homeward, circled in a necklace of fire, the complex thunder of artillery increased in tempo, shaking all creation.

Back at Ops. we learned, in the cryptic language of that branch, that the attack had achieved favourable cover with three flamers.

*   *   *

Day exploded dramatically at 0345 hours. It seemed that every weapon in the area was shouting defiance and filling the waning night with spectacular fireworks. For a brief moment I was reminded of the display that ended each day at the Exhibition. But when a heavy fall of flak stripped a nearby tent from its poles, the images of carnival vanished and were replaced by the alarming possibilities latent in the situation. The unseen raiders droned above us in the lively darkness. Ack-ack shells burst with sequin brilliance, like exploding nebulae in some distant universe, showering the night with cascades of lacy fire. Through this deadly embroidery stabbed the red-hot rods of tracers, searching the night for the target, rising in a slow evenly spaced sequence, like javelins hurled at Satan's invisible chariot. This infernal show, which lasted about forty minutes, made an end of sleep.

Even after the raiders had departed our own guns kept up a continuous drumming, and heavy enemy mortar fire jolted the area with sickening regularity. Around five o'clock our counter-battery shoot opened. By that hour we were supping coffee and preparing to witness the attack, if that were possible.

The morning was clear and still and heavy dew wet us to the knees as we made our way forward to the vantage point we had recced yesterday. The barrage was to come down at six minus three, or 0557 hours. Accompanying Hughes and me were Eric Harrison and Sergeant Powell, a staff writer for the divisional daily, *The Maple Leaf*. We watched the time anxiously as zero approached. Keeping close to the hedgerows, we came to the glade where the *scuole* stood. In its classrooms all the sinister preparations for the eventualities of battle were being hurriedly completed, the pungent smell of iodoform was strong in the morning air, stacks of rolled bandages awaiting the limbs and bodies shortly to be bound.

Our knoll had the advantage of a shell crater at its summit. We slid into its doubtful protection and looked about us. The Liri River was in a wooded depression on our left, the smoking town of Pontecorvo just ahead of us, with the line of poplars leading off to the right marking the road to Aquino and the Adolf Hitler Line. We were all conscious of the significance of the impending attack, the first major operation of the war wholly directed by a Canadian Corps. Our old friends, the 13th British Corps, had simulated an attack with great realism during the night, to divert enemy attention. How successful this had been would soon be known. In a few minutes now two Brigades of the 1st Division would be committed, supported by the 25th British Armoured Brigade. When their planned objectives had been reached, the 5th Canadian Armoured Division would pass through to the pursuit.

*   *   *

The Adolf Hitler Line is a carefully constructed and well considered defensive area, built by the Todt organization. It is not a continuous unbroken Maginot-style line, but a well planned series of powerful defensive localities, extending from the slopes of Monte Cairo on the east, passing through the towns of Aquino and Pontecorvo, and then tying in with the Aurunci massif on the west. Each of these localities are built around what is called a Panzertrum, a sort of miniature fort, looking for all the world as if a mark five Panther tank had been buried in concrete so that only the turret, the gun, and the traversing mechanism, appeared above the surface of the ground. The gun itself is a savage looking weapon, nineteen feet long, with brutal striking power. Around each locality is strung acres of wire, not the more obvious concertino wire, but an intricate barbed network close to the ground, hidden in the waving grass and crops. Outward from the wire are the mine fields, the tank ditches, and the built-in steel machine-gun pillboxes, ingeniously sited to bring down interlocking cross-fire on every possible line of approach. Since the great Panzertrum itself is immobile, except for its power to rotate on a traversing mechanism, anti-tank guns are employed as an additional mobile force. It appears to be their rôle to engage adventurous armour that might, in the heat of battle, elude the turret gun or attempt to outflank it. And since the turret gun has a relatively thin skin at its rear, it is extremely vulnerable when traversed to cover a flank. Behind these impressive impact weapons are the mortar platoons, with their multiple barrels, and then the sleek panzers themselves, each dark hull with its own lurking brood of grenadiers.

As the minute hand moved toward zero, we pondered the possible outcome of the impending battle. No one underestimated the power of the line we were attacking. We could see from the defence overprint map, which we carried, that if it were fully manned with determined forces, it would be the toughest battle Canadians had ever faced in any war. As zero passed, an iron cloud of dust and clangorous shock waves rose on all sides, and we found ourselves engulfed in the now-familiar environment of preposterous, inescapable sound. The troubled air above us was solid with the invisible passage of missiles. What went on beyond, in that obscure pavilion of dust, we could only guess. Black smoke from brew-ups and fuel fires mixed with it now, and a tongue of naked flame licked at the sky near the town.

We looked toward the Coufini plain on our right, from where the accent, if such there was, seemed to come. It was a flattish plain, divided by hedgerows, with scattered islands of low deciduous woods, a wretched site for a tank battle, no chance of a hulls-down approach, everything in the open with only an occasional slight screen of trees. From it rose a dense pallid cloud of dust and smoke, such as might rise from a forest fire. We could imagine the screaching clank of metal, the tear of sprocket and tread, as those great Churchills manoeuvred their vast bulk.

Beyond and away to the east was the blue silhouette of Monte Cairo, placid and indifferent to the struggle on the plain below. The vast contrast and conflict of responses created by the imagery about us was overwhelming.

Nineish the thunder slackened a bit. We had no way of knowing how the battle had gone, since our experience of it had been so limited. But we regarded it as a good moment to return to H.Q. On our way back a heavy shower of rain drenched the countryside.

*   *   *

The Liri first emerges from a high scree in the Simbruini. Fed by numberless little streams, it chatters and plunges down a deep mountain defile past the picturesque town of Sora, and then enters this beautiful and fertile valley. Almost immediately it comes into confluence with the Sacco and then, brimful, meanders gently in a southeasterly direction. Joined by the Melfa, it merges with the Rapido below Cassino. There, all the contributory streams lose their identity and the Garigliano flows serenly towards the Tyrrhenian Sea.

Viewed on a relief map this valley is a gigantic furrow paralleling the coast. It extends from just south of Cassino to the Alban hills. Once that attractive and historic obstacle is passed, it gives access to the Roman campagna by an inland route. Twenty-four centuries ago, when the Romans considered overland military communications with south Italy, they built the famous Via Appia, which traversed the Pontine marshes, rounded the coastal defile at Terracina, and then entered Capua over practically the same route as highway 7 today. The vital highway in this valley is Route 6, the Roman Via Latina. This great road connected the eternal city with ancient Casilinium. Today it is alternately referred to as the Via Casilina, or Route 6. Although it has not inherited the glamour of the Via Appia, it may be that its importance to the welfare of mankind has been underestimated. Undoubtedly the legions marched down the Via Casilina, but the beat of

ROCCA SAN GIOVANNI, LOOKING NORTH.

AQUINO, ITALY.

timpani and clatter of chariot wheels are more usually associated with the coastal road.

In this valley we are conscious of great teachers like
Benedict of Nursia, and Thomas of Aquino. When Benedict
left Subiaco there seems little doubt he and his followers
came down this valley and climbed the hill where he founded
the Abbey so recently destroyed. Seven centuries later a son
was born to the Count d'Aquino at his castle in Roccasecca,
about eight miles from our present location. Thomas of
Aquino spent his boyhood in this valley and received his
elementary education at the monastery on Monte Cassino.
Aquino itself, seat of the Count Landulf, his father, is one
of the nodal points of the Adolf Hitler Line, and must have
been crushed and burned, as Pontecorvo has been, within
the past forty-eight hours. Battle is not new to this valley,
but the blessings of peace have been a far more normal
experience throughout its long history.

*   *   *

There were long faces in the headquarters compound
when we returned. The silent tensions normal to men directing
a large scale attack were evident everywhere. Very little
reliable information was available and it was nearly midday
before we heard even the first rumours. No doubt the Ops
men were following the action closely, but it just did not
circulate to us. We had taken ninety prisoners . . . the 48th
Highlanders had suffered heavy casualties, B. Company, it
was rumoured, being particularly unfortunate . . . four out
of five officers were casualties, including Captain Wilson,
the company commander. This was very sad intelligence
and no doubt accounted for the solemn mien of the staff.

It was also rumoured that the enemy was massing a heavy
force of armour on our front. One informant reported that
he had 44 Mark IV and 24 Mark V tanks deployed between
the two roads leading out of Pontecorvo. Added to what he
was reported to have had last night, this would mean that

we were confronted with something approaching the might of a Panzer Division.

At 1430 hours we learned that it was now the intention to pass 3rd Brigade through 1st on our left flank, and then the entire 5th Canadian Armoured Division would pass through them and engage the enemy armour.

Drama mounted as the late afternoon sitreps* appeared. The great news was that the Adolf Hitler Line had been breached and that our forward troops continued to press across the Aquino-Pontecorvo road. A confirmed report was received, announcing that the attack had developed out of the Anzio bridgehead and that the Americans were advancing on the coastal strip beyond the mountains on our left. All of these pressures must have given the German High Command much to think about in the last few hours and it was not surprising to learn that they were withdrawing before our advance.

The tensions of the morning had passed and there was a feeling of jubilant excitement at Main 40. We were through the Adolf Hitler Line and there was a rumour that the Div. headquarters would move forward tomorrow. Lawren Harris came over from 5th Div. and shared a meal with us tonight.

*   *   *

Heavy ack-ack fire aroused us at 0310 hours. We looked out to see the night brilliant with magnesium flares. Struggling into rubber boots and trench coats, we made for the slit trench. The flak was intense and the sky seemed full of circling aircraft. Except for the flares, it was almost a repetition of the other night's show. Stars paled behind the amazingly red fire-play of thousands of tracer shells. Twenty yards away the road was jammed with our armour, moving steadily forward. The first indications of dawn were visible in the east before things quieted down a bit.

---

*Sitrep is the normal abbreviation used for "situation report."

Optimism ran high that morning. Seven hundred more prisoners had been brought in during the night and Cottam and the other interrogators were having a field day.

Invited early to make a reconnaissance of some of the German positions, we started out along the dusty towpath road leading to Pontecorvo. The verges and ditches were littered with German material of every description, anti-tank guns, unearthed and defused mines, nebelwerfer bombs, belts and belts of small arms ammunition, and signal wire in great confusion. Rounding a corner, we came upon one of the Panzertrum located beside the road. There was the great 7.5 cm. gun, protruding menacingly from its turret and surrounded by the wire obstacles we had heard so much about. The gun was traversed to one side, no doubt at the angle at which it had fired its last round. It now stood silent and abandoned in the bright sunlight, blackened by fire, and overlooking the Rione Campolato, a scene of dreadful havoc. From the top of the turret could be seen a huddle of brewed-up tanks, some Shermans, others the German Mark IV, mute but impressive evidence of the savage battle which had passed.

The axis of B. Company of the 48th Highlanders of Canada had been through these fields. The turret commanded a wide field of fire over the flat bottom-lands of the Liri at this point, and one could appreciate the grim nature of their task as one looked over the terrain. It was difficult to reconstruct the struggle as it occurred. Undoubtedly some of the Shermans had been victims of this gun, but it seemed possible too that they in turn had contributed to its destruction. In traversing to engage one of these tanks, this gun had been put out of action by a direct hit toward the rear of the turret, a hit evidently made by a six pounder anti-tank gun. Inside the turret were the grisly charred remains of the crew. We had been told that under these emplacements, in addition to ammunition magazines, were well-ventilated living quarters for the crew, with such extraordinary amenities as rabbit hutches and chicken coops for the storage of live rations, and chemical closets. We looked cautiously down into the dark interior, ready to accept the description without investigation.

Sappers were still defusing mines in order that tank recovery crews could tow out the serviceable hulls and it was extremely unhealthy to move about in areas not already swept. I made several pencil sketches, preparatory to more serious studies later.

On the Aquino road we visited other emplacements. In each case they had had their brief hour of tumultuous life and now stood destroyed and abandoned. The living combatants, with all the anxious haste of mechanized forces, had moved on, leaving these now useless engines, surrounded by the litter and debris of their own destructiveness, to gawk at one another. One gun created a fantastic sight, sticking perpendicularly up into the air, like a gigantic pylon memorializing the disasters of war. A direct hit had detonated its magazine, the resulting blast tearing the whole turret from its casemate and tossing it in the air. There it was, a vast, inert steel probe, blindly challenging the heavens. All about the battlefield were scattered derelict tanks. I counted fourteen confronting this one weapon, largely Churchills of the 25th Armoured Brigade.

*   *   *

Optimism was running high at Headquarters. The 5th Canadian Armoured Recce. was approaching the Melfa River, seven miles beyond Pontecorvo. In the morning they were across the river and closing in on the town of Ceprano.

Since Divisional Headquarters were on warning to move, we discussed the advisability of making sketches and reports on Cassino, before leaving the vicinity of that fateful town. It was thought that this might be possible, if we were back before evening. Harrison and I left immediately, accompanied by Hughes as far as Corps headquarters on the Cassino-Pignataro lateral.

This whole area had received the direct impact of our attack ten days ago and was a scene of destruction equal only in my experience to the Berardi sector on the Adriatic, with one striking difference, that the Berardi shelling took place in December and this had happened in May. The destruction of trees in full foliage creates a far more sinister impression of devastation than those destroyed in winter, seeming to evoke responses similar to those when a promising young life is suddenly and unexpectedly ended, symbolizing, in a sense, the disaster of human sacrifice which was taking place in this valley of shadow. No tree or shrub or bush along the road had escaped. They were stripped, shorn, shattered, and mutilated; the kill, in what foliage remained, lent to the landscape a shocking, late autumnal, colour.

Pignataro itself was a typical lifeless rubble pile. The inhabitants were either dead or had been evacuated. The dust of the bombardment, and from the numberless hurrying vehicles, had given the wreckage a flour-bin pallor. A monument to the Italian fallen of the First World War, in what had been the main square, was blasted from its pedestal, leaving only one jagged bronze leg high on its base, the heroic pointing figure standing canted in the dusty rubble, pointing with super-realistic irony at the passing soldiery.

The Benedictine monastery, topping its high hill, still dominated the valley impressively. As we approached more closely, the wasted desolation of its proud ruin became more apparent and one found it difficult to understand why so great a monument should have been destroyed by our own generation. We had had no opportunity to examine very closely the circumstances which had made the bombing a military necessity. No doubt there had been very real provocation, but in eliminating a military problem western culture had lost a great monument of art, and an institution which had contributed vitally to its life for nearly fourteen hundred years. The parts of the abbey destroyed three months before included rich accretions of the art of the sixteenth, seventeenth and eighteenth centuries. The central court was traditionally attributed to Donato Bramante. From the central court-yard, by way of a wide flight of steps, one entered a court attributed to Antonio de San Gallo the younger. Contrasted with the simple, fine lines of the cloisters was the extra-ordinary baroque richness of the interior of the church. Everywhere had been splendours of all kinds, inlaid marbles, sculptures, pictures, stuccos, gold work, wood carving. The vault of the church was decorated with frescoes by Luca Giordano. Conca had painted the interior of the chapels. One trembled to think of the appalling loss because it was obviously all gone. We were hopeful that the library might have been evacuated before the bombing. Certainly the fixed architectural features of this remarkable building were gone beyond recall.

Rounding the monastery hill, Cassino itself came into view. For sheer horror and utter devastation, I had not set eyes on its equal. The terraced structure of the streets might be discerned, if one searched for structure in that formless heap of calcined stone, but it resembled rather some imagined landscape on the moon. It had ceased to be terrestrial, it was like some lidless, blind eye, glaring back at the sun with empty lifeless inertia.

The town in itself was completely silent. Swallows darted aimlessly about, their plaintive shriek the only sound other than the roll of gunfire and the clatter of armour. Unburied dead, protruding from rubble or huddled grotesquely in cellars, still made a grisly spectacle. The heavy stench of corruption hung about in dense patches near the pile of debris that was once the Hotel des Roses. In the flats, near the Rapido River, the lands flooded by the enemy bristled with shattered tree stumps, the stagnant surface dull with a heavy brownish algae. Streets were no longer streets, simply tiresome mountains of broken masonry, in some instances reaching to second-storey levels. The Pinnacle, a cone-shaped feature topped by the mediaeval ruin of Rocca Ianula, where the New Zealanders had paid so dearly, overlooked desolation on all sides. The Roman amphitheatre, the Cappella del

Crocifisso, the luxurious Continental, the Baron's Palace,
all were reduced to a common denominator. What had been
gardens were whittled to the ground, thick stumps of palm
torn and gashed, vines uprooted, unidentifiable trees chopped
and shattered into kindling. The ground everywhere was
strewn with shell fragments, spent casings, and a litter of
German equipment. In a most depressed state of mind, I set
up my equipment to one side of Route 6 and sketched what
was left of the town.

* * *

Divisional Headquarters moved north to Pofi in two
bounds. The spirit revives with movement, in such a situation,
and lively excitement filled the camp as we harboured our
vehicles in a barley field. The enemy was in headlong retreat.
2nd Canadian Infantry Brigade had liberated Frosinone, and
elements of the 5th American Army were engaging the enemy
heavily a mile from Valmontone. If they were successful in
breaching Route 6 south of that point, the four German
divisions in this valley would be in an embarrassing position.

Hughes and I wandered over to a nearby irrigation
reservoir and had a refreshing swim in delightfully chill water.
We had been in convoy all day, seated in an open jeep, and
looked as if we had just knocked off shift at a gypsum
factory. It had been a still hot morning, following a night
filled with the roar and clank of moving armour as the
advance party of the 6th South African Armoured Division
moved into the area. The road was hidden in dust as we
edged into the northbound convoy and came to an immediate
standstill. In the first hour we advanced half a mile, at the
end of the second we were two and one-half miles from the
start, and so it went on all day. Churchills were passing continuously through grain fields on our right, and the enormous
dust-cloud they created drifted over the road and hovered
before settling on the convoy. The tanks wore the red patch
of the 1st Canadian Division and bore such brave battle
names as "Blenheim," "Malplaquet," "Ramillies," "Corunna,"

etc. At the end of the third hour we had gone less than three miles and overlooked the confluence of the Melfa and Liri rivers, a mile wide flats with a line of vehicles, bumper-to-tailboard, winding down to the ford. After four hours we had done three miles.

The midday sun was dazzling as we descended in our dustcloud onto the floor of the valley and sat awaiting our turn to negotiate the crossing. The Melfa is a wide stony watercourse with the muddy stream running to one side, about as wide as the Don. We remained in this hot valley an endless time, unable to move far from our vehicles. It was risky, in any case, to move beyond the white tapes. By mid-afternoon we had passed around the outskirts of Ceprano and toward evening we saw the Commandant, Captain Duncan Drummond Young, directing us into the barley field. Like other roadside grain fields, it was patterned with dwarfish, frumpy mulberry trees, between which grape vines spread trailing tendrils along wire supports.

*   *   *

We had returned from Cassino in a hurry, fearful of missing the Divisional move, only to wait twenty-four hours for it to begin. I was grateful for the break because I had really been shaken by what I had experienced there. But news of the operation was good. There were unrestrained expressions of joy when it was announced that the American 6th Corps had contacted the bridgehead at Anzio. Fierce fighting was proceeding in Cisterna. We learned too that our recce was then forward of that reach of the Liri which traverses our axis. But concurrently with this good news there were, as always, unconfirmed rumours concerning the fate of many fine men, that Captain Norman Pope of the Seaforths of Vancouver, and Captain Conway, for instance, had been lost, both magnificent chaps, popular with everyone. A silent depression took over, not dispelled even when the facts were known: Captain Conway had been very seriously wounded and might lose his right arm; Captain Pope had been L.O.B'd.

The move, when it came on the 27th, was only a matter of five miles, but it involved the gruesome passage through the ghost town of Pontecorvo. The town had been a nodal point in the enemy's defence line and had taken an awful beating. It had been muck-raked by artillery fire, and air-bombed for days, with the usual catastrophic results. The convoy was not a fast one, since the narrow rubble-piled streets were a defile through which every vehicle had to pass in single file, giving us all ample time to view in comprehensive detail the work of gangs of Italian labourers, clearing up the mess. Corpses being removed from the rubble for burial, bloody, stiffened, waxen forms, lay about in a gagging stench, some pressed into grotesque corrugations describing the dreadful shape and pressures of the masonry that had crushed them, others severed and mutilated beyond all semblance of humans. We were relieved to leave the town behind and enter the more bearable environment of dust and heat.

Our campsite north of Pontecorvo was for the first time in a field of grain, bearded wheat, I think it was, or possibly barley. Our tent was under a giant oak bordering the field and a shallow, dry streambed offered excellent cover nearby. Sherman tanks were dispersed under nets in the waving grain and offered a dynamic subject for a painting, which I undertook the moment we became settled.

The engines were silent but the crews rested in readiness in the shade of the hulls. The closest tank was of the 12th Canadian Armoured Regiment, Three Rivers, commanded by Corporal Trueman of Toronto. While I worked we received the tragic news that our C.R.E., Lieut-Colonel K. S. "Ken" Southern had been killed, a blow that tried us all heavily. While making a reconnaissance for possible crossings of the Melfa his jeep had touched off a mine, killing him and his wireless operator, seriously wounding his driver. Hughes, who knew Colonel Southern well, was particularly shocked when he learned the news, on his return from 2nd Brigade, himself the bearer of other tragic news. Among others, Lieut-Brown-Clayton was missing, possibly killed, an old messmate of ours from Campobasso days, a sensitive and wonderful boy. We have successfully breached the Adolf Hitler Line, but many Canadians we have known well and admired are no longer with us.

*   *   *

On Thursday morning, June 1st, our makeshift mess at Pofi shook with loud debate; it had to be loud to be heard. Churchills and Shermans still roared by on the dusty road, while ten yards away a Field Battery was dealing out salvos of harrassing fire.

It was a day of burning stillness, filled with dust, noise, and oppressive heat. Pofi was a bleak little town on a ridge, possibly a mile away, a great square belfry or campanile dominating the skyline. There were no olives in the district and very few grapes, it seemed to be a mixed farming community with light deciduous woods, but even through the dust and martial noises could be seen a lovely pastoral countryside. We had been given short notice to move but when we left the campsite we were under the impression that we were bound for an area in the vicinity of Frosinone. To our surprise, but not our sorrow, we had been directed into another grain field, half a mile from Ceccano on the Sacco River.

Rome, June:

Rome was liberated on the 4th of June. On the night of the 3rd, and for some time before, I had been suffering from a rather common complaint which afforded me unusual opportunities for experiencing the beauties of the Italian summer night. I remember a biscuit-coloured moon, staring silently from a warm velvety sky, strange birds chattering and piping in the night. One sounded like a bank clerk stamping cancelled cheques, another like a man whistling to his dog. Then there was the inevitable "B.B.C. Bird" (the Nightjar) and the liquid brilliance of the nightingale.

The morning of the 4th was burning hot. Ceccano, to the west of us, was a vaporous fantasy on its beehive hill, topped by a grim crenellated tower. Below, the Sacco flowed around the ragged stumps of the piers that once carried a bridge. The still air carried the distant rumble of gunfire and, closer at hand, the occasional echoing blast of a teller mine. An early rumour vaguely suggested that the American 88th Div. had entered Rome. After lunch this rumour persisted but "G" Intelligence would not confirm it. We received the news with satisfaction, but not with the wild enthusiasm that might have been expected. The fall of Rome was something 1st Div. had considered as a possibility six months before. Now that it was imminent and inevitable, it had lost none of its importance, but its facination for us had dwindled with the likelihood of our own participation less certain.

On the morning of June 5th, it was confirmed that Rome had been entered by Allied Forces on the previous day. No doubt the "I" staff had known this, but even at a divisional headquarters it takes time for news of this character to percolate to peripheral sections like our own. Now that we were reconciled to the part our formation would not play in this stirring event, we were able to discuss the situation with more objectivity. Obviously the war was entering a climactic phase, a point of view confirmed on this day by the first tremor of the action impending in Normandy. It was rumoured that the second front would be opened sometime between the 5th and the 15th, a suggestion which created far greater excitement than had the liberation of Rome.

I turned my attention to my duties. If this was to be our furthest north, I must make a painting of Ceccano in the Lazio. It was a dreadfully hot day, about ninety, I should say. I drove four bamboo canes into the stubble of a grain field, stretched an Italian ground sheet over them, and under this improvised shelter, started to paint.

* * *

At 0800 hours on the 6th June, the signals truck broadcast the B.B.C. news over a loudspeaker. Shouts rose and men hurried from all points of the encampment. The German radio had admitted that the Allied invasion of Normandy had started earlier that morning. Tremendous excitement prevailed, temporarily eclipsing the depression caused by the announcement that we were to go into army reserve. At last the second front . . . We had no idea of the scale of the action, or what success had attended the assault phase, but there had been plenty of conjecture about the number of divisions that would be committed and the aircraft involved. A day of wild excitement followed, with unprecedented celebration in the mess at lunch time.

* * *

We entered the great city through the Porta Maggiore. As we crossed the wide expanse of the Piazzale we began to feel more at ease. We had arrived. Here we were in the bright Roman sunshine, already receiving the friendly greetings of the citizens.

Sixty miles of driving in an open jeep along the dusty Via Casilina had lent to the three of us the appearance of circus clowns. The fact that the Provost were turning back all but British and American vehicles had forced us to turn down and cover our windscreen, hiding the Division's tactical sign. This enforced deception had lent to our arrival not only excitement but the added quality of stealth. But now, in the Via Principe Eugenio, roses and oleander blossoms were thrown into our jeep and we were slowed to a walk by the happy milling crowds. Handshakes, smiles, bunting, and blown kisses greeted our dusty presence on all sides. We forgot the Provost and the tensions of the journey.

My first impressions were of the overwhelming beauty of a well-groomed city, gleaming in the bright summer sunshine. Since I left Montreal I had not seen a modern city which had escaped being crushed and burned, and the fact that I had recently passed through Cassino intensified the ordered beauty of the Piazza Vittorio Emanuele.

The Via Nazionale was hung with flags. The red, white and green stirred languidly in the hot sunshine, beside Old Glory and the Union Jack. An Italian city intact. It was wonderful to behold, it was more than that, it was an international metropolis, for many the spiritual capital of Christendom. Here it was, undamaged.

Harrison was keen to see as much of the city as our brief visit would permit, but he had two immediate ambitions: to stand under Mussolini's balcony, and to immerse himself in the Tiber! Possibly the one was an act of purification after indulging in the other. We swung down the Via Novembre IV into the crowded Piazza Venezia and drew up alongside the Palazzo in good campaign style. In spite of our rather desperate appearance, thanks to the cordiality of our welcome, we had recovered our composure.

*   *   *

It was just after one in the afternoon of the 7th when we drew up in the shadow of the Palazzo Venezia. Before we wiped the dust from our faces I asked O'Neil, my driver, to take a picture of Eric and me sitting in the jeep. The Piazza was bright with banners and bunting, and noisy with the hubbub of Allied troops and transports. To the vast curiosity of the Roman populace, a Highland pipe band skirled down the west side of the square, their tasselled sporans swinging to the measure of their step. Two gigantic Italian flags hung from the twin poles in front of the blinding whiteness of the Vittorio Emanuele Memorial. High up in that frosty structure I could see the tiny figures of two Italian soldiers, mounting guard beside the tomb of Italy's Unknown Warrior of the

First World War. Closer at hand, the great black doors of the Palazzo had chalked on them "Mussolini e morte" and a swastika had a huge cross struck violently through its centre. Above hung the celebrated balcony, now sombre and empty.

The whole scene had an unreal dream-like quality about it. I recalled an evening in this same great square just five years before, during the 'sanctions crisis,' when the crowds were chanting "Duce! Duce! Duce!" endlessly and in unison, until it seemed that even the paving stones trembled underfoot, while I, a Canadian onlooker, chose prudently to remain silent and anonymous. The play and most of the actors had changed on this bright sunny afternoon. My role was no longer silent or anonymous. In fact everything had changed, except the stage on which the play was taking place. . .

After an Army Rations lunch converted into a banquet by a carafe of white Frascate wine, we considered our position carefully. After all, we did have to be back at our Headquarters for tomorrow's movement. But being still unwashed, the enemy having thoughtfully and effectively eliminated water, light and power facilities, Harrison was bent on immersing himself in the Tiber. So, in that direction and with the utmost difficulty, we threaded our way. Not only the sidewalks, but the narrow lanes themselves, were thronged with soldiers and civilians, bound in every direction, utterly heedless of the risk they ran as the equally heedless army vehicles appeared to plough through them.

Suddenly the staggering impact of Salvi's Fontana di Trevi burst upon us and compelled us to stop and delight in the mythical splendours of the river god. Were we not on our way to join him in his kingdom, and was not this imperious Neptune himself, in his winged chariot, preceded by giant conch-blowing Tritons, overlooking the noisy crowd? We sought his indulgence and protection and proceeded through the Piazza di Spagna, replete with flowers and flower-girls, even as I had seen it last. Here we spoke to a very chic American woman who, with her Italian husband, volunteered

to direct us to a "bagni publico" on the river, if we would
drive them through the mob to their home. Such was contrary
to regulations, but then we were celebrating a great event.
Their house was pretentious, on the Lungo Tevere near the
Littoria Bridge, the German escape bridge, so they told us.
We were not invited in, a rebuff which deflated us considerably, but of course we did look disreputable, and we were
unwashed.

Crossing to the Scala di Pinedo, we found a floating
bath-house moored to the river bank. In a very few minutes
we had entrusted our perspiring bodies to the bosom of the
Tiber and the wiles of the river god.

We plunged and cavorted in the chilly waters in faded
blue draw-string trunks. They must have been worn by
enemy troops the week before. This was a rare form of
relaxation in a theatre of war, and swimming in the Tiber
still rarer. We thoroughly indulged our pale bodies. Harrison
had all the appearances of a sculptural freak with a bronze
head stuck on a marble torso, the knees and forearms gilded
as an afterthought. Though we were regarded with great
curiosity, no one joined us in the beige waters and, after a
suitable period of sunning on the deck of the bath-house,
feeling much refreshed, we resumed our tour.

Crossing the Ponte San Angelo, we turned along the
Lungotevere toward St. Peters. Instead of choirs of angels
and seraphim filling the air with celestial music, the familiar
thunder of tank engines, intensified by the grinding clank of
metal tracks on stone causeway, smote our ears. In single file
an endless column of Shermans roared in a penumbra of dust
across the Piazza Rusticucci, their slender radio antennae
swaying beside goggled and helmetted young men who
emerged with the impassiveness of charioteers from the crew
hatches. This Martian pandemonium was in strange contrast
to the gentle cause of the shrine that lay beyond it.

Vatican City was barricaded by a wooden fence; a sign
announced "Neutral Territory." There, through the glittering
spray from the fountains, was the majesty of the great dome,

like a crowned sun rising above the balustrade of the portico, preceded by Christ and his apostles, pleading with humanity for grace and understanding. Peter and Paul stood silently in timeless dignity on their separate pedestals, against a background of columns like giant sequoias upholding the mighty pediment.

Crossing the threshold of the church, we left behind the world of pitiless heat and sound and entered the relative quiet of the nave. The astounding scale of Bramante's conception is still supreme as the eye soars to the sunlight illuminating the collar above the great domed crossing. Magnificent as is the baroque lining, I like mentally to strip it away and see the travertine structure itself as Julius and Michelangelo saw it, austere possibly, but a daring triumph of monumental simplicity.

Harrison stood silently for a long time, gazing about him. He had not previously seen the church and, with the quiet temperance of Anglo-Saxon taste, he found Bernini's elegant decoration most disquieting. I attempted to calm him by leading him to the vicinity of the Michelangelo "Pieta." With this discovery his mood improved, his expression softened and he engaged in the most humane and kindly observations concerning that masterpiece. In this frame of mind we approached the Baldacchino, Harrison recalling Montaigne's criticism of ceremonies and their trappings as foreign to the purpose and cause of worship. He recoiled from the ascending whorles of the massive bronze columns as if they had been serpents, and thought that the metal might better have been left on the roof of the Pantheon.

But it was getting late and the prospect of the impending movement of the Corps next day forced us to move with irreverent haste. We looked up into that mighty vaulted dome which hung poised in the sky of the Urbs, the Evangelists crying their message from the pendentives; it was good to see it intact. In the "Tribuna" the four gigantic saints still held St. Peter's throne above the high altar. We passed a succession of elaborate Papal Tombs, Pollaiuolo's monument to Innocent VIII, I think it is, Della Porta's Tomb of Paul III. Our hobnails clattered on the marble floor as we passed the great baroque fonts and out once more into the blinding Roman sunshine. We had literally walked once round the nave, no time for the chapels or the apartments. But after all, we were fortunate to be making this visit on borrowed time.

We left the Piazza de Trionfi in the dark at a quarter to ten and made our exit from the city as we had entered it, through the Porta Maggiore. It was decided that I should drive for the first hour, before turning over to O'Neill. Happily, the Via Canlina was empty and we made excellent time. With any sort of luck we should be back in our lines soon after midnight. We were all a bit tired and the night was cool after the furnace heat of the day. Valmontone fell behind and then we started meeting traffic, 15 cwt's to begin with, then three-tonners. Finally, to my horror, we heard the thunder of Armour approaching. We were obliged to slow down, make frequent stops, and then about midnight halt for fully half an hour. Little conversation passed between us as the enthusiasms of the day cooled in the night air. O'Neill, who was then driving, managed to get us into the town of Ferrantino where British provost signalled us to the roadside and there we bogged down completely at about one o'clock. Tanks of the 6th Armoured Brigade descended on us in a continuous stream. The red caps could tell us nothing beyond the fact that this was a high priority movement and that no south-bound traffic would be permitted to pass beyond Ferrantino until the column had cleared their checkpoint. Our spirits sank in despair and, being dog-tired, we quaked with cold.

*　　　*　　　*

Leaving St. Peter's, we had accepted the hospitality of "S" Force at the Albergo Quirinale and, fortified by their kindness, discussed the use of the brief time that remained.

From the Campidoglio we walked slowly down the uneven causeway of the Via di Foro Romano into the velvety solitude of the ruins, great warm silhouettes against a pale melon-coloured sky. I suppose they had never been so silent since the middle ages. It was an odd pastoral sort of silence; swallows wheeled about; a sandy-coloured cat listened intently to the evening birdsong. Except for us, the Forum was utterly deserted. Oleander bloomed in white and a rather violent cerise, acanthus curved greenly out of the earth. But the silence of the place was almost oppressive as we wandered about, saying little.

The arch of Septimus Severus seemed massive in the half-light. The two large basilicas, Julia and Aemilia, were bricked up. The tumble of columns recalled Piranese's prints, or Giovanni Panini's paintings. Harrison talked of the Gens Julia-Claudia family, and of the Augustian propensity for collecting Egyptian obelisks. Those that once stood in the Circus Maximus are still to be found in Rome; one, I know, centres the Piazzo del Popolo. The arches of Titus and of Constantine are heavily enclosed in protective masonry. There, of course, was Flavian's Amphitheatre, the Maple Leaf Gardens of ancient Rome. But time was running out and it was getting dark. We had agreed to meet O'Neill in the Piazza di Trionfi at twenty-one thirty hours and it was already that hour. We had seen Rome in the hour of her liberation, in June 1944.

* * *

We remained halted in Ferrantino. Armour clanked through the dusty rubble-filled streets in endless procession. I tried to sleep in the back seat, Harrison in the front, but jeeps are not designed for sleeping. O'Neill found a table in a wrecked bakery nearby. But there was no rest and, as the others pointed out, in spite of my presence, no comfort.

The east paled around four o'clock and we walked about and beat our arms to restore our failing circulation. We had left the day previously in a hurry, dressed in shorts and cotton shirts, utterly unprepared for a night in the open. Of course it could have been worse; at 0430 hours there was a lull that wakened us completely. The clangour of the last Sherman died away as it lumbered down the curving hill behind us. The Red Caps signalled us through with malicious smiles on their faces. It had amused them to witness our misery and helplessness. Paralyzed with cold, we straightened up and returned their salute without betraying, or so we thought, the slightest sign of distress or inconvenience caused by our night in Ferantino.

Rome, July:

Yesterday the temperature had been one hundred and one in the shade. Although it was still before nine in the morning, the early oppressiveness suggested that there would be no surcease from the heat today. I mopped my brow as we drove down the Via della Conciliazione toward the vast embrace of Bernini's colonnade.

Colonel Gilchrist, freshly shaved, and attired in a crisply laundered shirt, sat beside me, fanning himself with a sheaf of galley-proofs. "Once we get inside, away from this sun, we will be all right," he said, as we alighted at the foot of the long triple gradient of steps, leading to the shelter of the Basilica. The refracted sunlight seared and the wonders of that vast piazza seemed to burn like a fiery cross, as we mounted the steps to the deep shade of the portico.

Once inside, expressions of relief escaped us both. It was like escaping from a western blizzard, in reverse. Having established our identities with the Swiss Guard and communicated with the Vatican authorities who were expecting us, we entered the sacred precincts. The vast nave was positively chill at this hour. A vague amber light, plus a subtle fragrance of incense, mellowed the overwhelming multiple impact of its mighty decor.

I had driven to Rome from Divisional Headquarters at Piedmonte D'Aliffe with orders to sketch the High Mass to be celebrated in St. Peter's for the Royal 22nd Regiment on July 3rd. Gilchrist was to write the story of this great occasion for the Canadian Army daily in Italy, *The Maple Leaf.* Absorbed in his assignment, he was saying, "I must try to see O'Flaherty. I shall return here well before ten and contact you before the Mass begins." With that, he bore off to the left and disappeared.

The Basilica had attracted large numbers of troops this morning, many more than were here a month earlier. Many were worshippers, others moved in groups, sampling, like bees in a summer garden. They had no guides, they needed none. They looked with unconcealed wonder at the mosaicized version of Domenichino's painting of the "Communion of Saint Jerome," or at the same treatment of Raphael's "Transfiguration," at the rich marble panelling, the porphyry sarcophagi, the melanchy romanticism of Canova's carving, or the rigid bronze statue of Saint Peter, with its toe worn bright by the lips of the faithful.

Was the Basilica really the exaggerated and excessive expression which so many northerners feel it to be? I was inclined to think not, no more so than any dream. Surely this is a very great dream, that has been realized and can be appreciated by all who possess imagination, regardless of their faith. There are, of course, many details which one does not personally like, yet the total effect is one of tumultuous, triumphant inventiveness, in the presence of which personal tastes should, at all times, be qualified by a sense of historic fitness. After all, Gian Lorenzo Bernini is the principal decorator.

A procession emerged into the nave from the right, a mixed group of civilians and soldiers suddenly attracted toward it. At first I could see only clusters of lighted tapers, moving ever so slowly toward the papal altar, evoking that quality of passionate mysticism one associates with certain forms of *lirico-majico* painting. Soberly dressed women fell on their knees, some even wept, as six Ethiopians, clad in richly embroidered emerald green vestments, moved in twos, each bearing a cluster candelabra of lighted tapers. Faces and hands not being discernible, they created an illusion of lighted candles preceding green vestments, by virtue of some mystical propulsion. Liveried attendants appeared to follow, then came two brilliant Cardinals, rustling in their crimson robes, one a kindly white-haired figure with tortoise-shell glasses whom I had seen before in Vatican ceremonies. These dazzling princes walked with solemn dignity, side by side, extending their hands to right and left so that the kneeling supplicants might kiss their rings. The most surprising and unexpected part of the procession then came into view, an open casket of crimson, carried by six pallbearers in such a way that the recumbent figure of the deceased might readily be seen. In the casket lay exposed the mortal remains of Giuseppe Sarto who, as Pope Piux X, died on the 20th August, 1914, nearly thirty years ago.

Giuseppe Sarto had lived through the great revolutionary period of Italian history. He had seen Austria lose the greater part of her Italian possessions to the flourishing new Kingdom. At the same time, he had seen the Papal State occupied, first by Garibaldi, and then by Victor Emmanuel, and finally merged into the Kingdom of Italy. He had a reputation for simplicity and humble piety, which may have accounted for the veneration and respect being paid to his remains on this occasion.

As the casket approached, impressive and moving demonstrations of veneration and profound sorrow occurred among those witnessing the procession. The dead Pope wore his mitre and robes, and on his crimson-gloved hand shone a great jewelled ring. His face, the colour of old parchment, possessed a serene calm, the dignified and regular features appearing well preserved and obviously identifiable to the many elderly Italians who knelt and made efforts to touch some part of the Papal garments. Although I had no knowledge of the purpose or significance of the ceremony, I found myself somehow moved by what I saw. The procession crossed the nave and entered a side chapel, still led by the flickering candles.

Shortly before ten, I saw General Georges Vanier, approaching up the long nave from the front of the Basilica, the jerky step imposed by his artificial limb making his identity unmistakable. He was accompanied by Brigadier Paul Bernatchez and the Padre of the Royal 22nd.

They were shown simple chairs at the left of the high altar in the Tribune, three tiny mortals, seated under that over-whelming baroque reredos. The mystic dove of the Holy Ghost shone in an aura of golden light, surrounded by circling hosts of cherubim. Above the gigantic throne of Peter, two seraphim held between them the Vicar's triple tiara, and in their other hands the great keys to paradise. This stupendous altar of the Cathedra Petri formed the mighty backdrop behind the three Canadians. They themselves looked toward the great doors, through which the Regiment was shortly to approach.

General Vanier had flown to Rome from Algiers, expressly for this great occasion and now sat, erect and imposing, below the massive throne of St. Peter, awaiting the rank and file of the unit he had once commanded. A great soldier and a born diplomat, General Vanier had come to be regarded as Canada's perennial ambassador to the French Republic, and how ably he has filled that post, a friendly, genial individual, at the same time the personification of dignity. During these anxious days he was representing us at Algiers, where the Government of the French Republic was carrying on its responsibilities in temporary exile.

At ten o'clock I heard the crash of marching feet, striking the marble pavement of the nave with a harsh beat. The echoes in the Basilica were fantastic as they reached up into the dome itself and then found their way down again to merge loudly in a sort of rhythmic gibberish with the original tread. Lieutenant-Colonel Jean Allard looked a heroic figure as he

led his men past the whorling baldichino, toward the high
altar where they formed up in five columns of three ranks,
facing the altar, and the Mass commenced.

$$*\qquad\qquad*\qquad\qquad*$$

As the Mass progressed I worked rapidly on pencil notes
from a precarious position at the base of one of the vast piers
which support the dome. In spite of this slightly elevated
position, it was difficult for me to sketch. Literally hundreds
of visitors to the Basilica had become interested witnesses to
the Mass and, unfortunately for me, had bunched themselves
between my position and the worshipping troops. These dense
moving groups of non-participating observers included scores
of Moslems and Buddhists from the Indian Divisions of the
8th Army, watching the ceremony with curious but respectful
interest. Many of them were big bearded men who, though
in themselves picturesque and interesting, quite effectively
blocked my vision.

The nave was particularly colourful as I gazed about at
its staggering detail. The pilasters of the apse were hung
with red damask trimmed with gold. This had been part of
the recent ceremonial decoration of the church in honour of
St. Peter himself, who is celebrated annually on June 29th.
On that occasion the Pope had celebrated Mass under the
great baldichino on my right. It must have been a majestic
sight with the altar surrounded by the ninety-five gilded lamps
burning the Gethsemane oil. On that occasion too, the ancient
bronze statue of the Saint, attributed by some to Arnolfo di
Cambio, was crowned with the mitre, robed in episcopal
vestments, and venerated by thousands.

The Mass was now reaching its climax. I had by this time
been forced to abandon my sketching and join the great
throng of witnesses, in order to imbibe the last bit of colour
from the scene. Colonel Gilchrist now joined me and the
Royal 22nd Regiment disappeared from view. High above
the altar, before which they had worshipped, I could see the

massive Chair of St. Peter, supported by the colossal bronze
statues of the four doctors of the church, Saints Augustine,
Ambrose, Athanasius, and John Chrysostom. We made our
way slowly down the nave and out into the sunshine.

*   *   *

The mid-summer heat lay heavy and thick in the Roman
streets. The reservoirs at Tivoli had not yet been repaired
and dust and papers replaced the cooling splash of water in
countless fountains. The Tiber stirred languidly around the
bridge abutments, dense, opaque, torpid, and, no doubt, as
hot as lentil soup. The breath of the tall pines in the Borghese
gardens seemed to come from a brasier, and the cats, sunning
around the Pantheon, clawed savagely, even at shadows.

I replaced my beret and adjusted my sunglasses as I
descended the steps of Santa Maria della Vittoria and crossed
the Piazza d'Esedra to the deep shade of the Via Nazionale.
I had had a disappointment. I am not particularly a Bernini
enthusiast, in fact much of baroque architecture and sculpture
is a bit rich for my simple tastes, but then who can help but
admire the tumultuous creations of that irrepressible spirit.
The church itself is small, a rather good example of the more
restrained style of Carlo Moderna. There was a high
catafalque before the Domenichino altar, draped in purple
and gold, and the heavy fragrance of incense that hung in the
warm air announced rather obviously that funeral rites had
recently taken place. But what I was unprepared for was the
fact that the St. Theresa chapel was entirely bricked up. At
first I thought I had made some mistake, but then I realized,
as I had yesterday, that this was protective masonry, and that
somewhere, hidden behind the bricks was the ecstatic Saint
swooning like a love-sick maiden. I had seen her in the days
before the war, but I like to return and test earlier impressions
against the passage of time. Shored up behind her brick wall,
Theresa was safe alike from bombs and the appraising eyes
of sceptics and philistines, and I was grateful to the authorities

who had taken these sensible precautions to protect so interesting a monument, at the same time that I was disappointed.

Yesterday I had had a similar experience when I went to
San Pietro in Vincoli to see, among other things, the Michelangelo Moses. I have always felt that this noble prophet
appears impatient with the dull task of sitting eternally on
the Della Rovere tomb. Toying with his beard he gazes
wistfully toward the door of the church, wishing he could
rise and walk out into the sunshine. At least these had been
my impressions; I was quite ready to discard them. I walked
through the empty church to the site of the tomb of Julius,
to find, to my astonishment a great buttress of brick and
mortar concealing the entire monument. It was a disappointment, but with compensations, and I realized that although I
had been denied the pleasure on this occasion, Moses would
be there next time, and no doubt when my grandchildren visit
Rome.

*   *   *

O'Neil and I had just left the Latern church and were
about to pass in front of the San Giovanni gate when a
dilapidated and overcrowded bus rattled and clanked to a stop
directly in front of our jeep. Though we could have backed
up and gone the other way, there was something about this
bus and its vast burden of humanity which fascinated us. They
were obviously refugees in transit, no doubt from the
battle-stricken areas to the south of Rome, on their way to
join relatives and friends here or further north. They were
burdened with a great miscellany of the customary minor
possessions, boxes, bags, baby carriages, bird cages, musical
instruments and, of course, numerous hungry and tired
children.

While we watched a distracted adult attempt to console
a very unhappy small boy, a matronly figure in a nurses' white
uniform approached us from the bus, shouting "Hello there,
Canada!" We were a little taken aback to be addressed with
such easy and friendly familiarity, but it became clear that

it was help she wanted and O'Neil carried her weighty suitcase to the safety island beside the jeep. When she came up to the vehicle I could see that she was a handsome elderly woman with wisps of greying hair escaping from under her flowing white headdress. The red cross was conspicuous and on her bosom was a row of tattered World War I ribbons, including the Allied Victory medal. "I am so glad to see you here. Would you be going anywhere near the Piazza del Popolo?" O'Neil and I looked at one another. It was forbidden to transport civilians in A.A. vehicles, but clearly she was in uniform and was not a civilian. We hesitated only a moment before O'Neil, on a raised eye-brow, climbed into the back of the jeep with the suitcase. "That probably could be arranged, Madam," said I, and up she climbed beside me. "I saw you were Canadians. I gave a lecture in Ottawa in 1937." We swept out of the Piazza and down the Via San Giovanni in Laterano, past San Clemente and round the Colosseum. "I don't think I heard your name, Madam," I said. "My name is Garibaldi," said she, fumbling in her purse. "I am a granddaughter of Giuseppe Garibaldi!"

I pulled in to the curb on the Via dell Impero. She had found a letter she wanted me to read and I wanted to take another look at my passenger. It is not every day one picks up a close relative of Giuseppe Garibaldi, even in Italy. "This is my card, which you may have, and here is a letter from your Prime Minister!" The card said "Anita T. Garibaldi, Via Pompeo Magno 1," the letter, dated at Ottawa, came from the Office of the Prime Minister and was signed "Yours sincerely, W. L. Mackenzie King." It dealt with the distinct pleasure her visit to Canada had afforded him and with his hope that they might meet again in the future. "What was the purpose of your visit to Ottawa, may I ask?" "I had been invited to lecture there on the life of my grandfather." He and the grandfather of Mackenzie King were not unlike in character I thought, detesting political dishonesty and corruption they fought for responsible government in their respective countries. As we travelled with the windscreen

down over the hood, the white veil streamed out behind like
a club burgee and everyone seemed appropriately interested
in the spectacle. "To get to my apartment we cross the
Margherita Bridge here."

As we swept round the Piazza del Popolo, the involved
pattern of two extraordinary lives took vague form in my
mind. I remembered my absorption with William Lyon
Mackenzie ten years ago when we were preparing material
for the brochure which celebrated Toronto's centenary. At
that time I had reconstructed a portrait of the rebellious old
patriot who, incidentally, had been the first Mayor of Toronto
in 1835. I had never met his grandson, but here beside me
was Anita T. Garibaldi, telling me that she had not been to
the ancestral home at Caprera in Sardinia for many years. . .
We turned off the Lungotevere Michelangiolo, and there was
her Roman home. The contact was all too exciting and too
brief. O'Neil and I accompanied her to the door. We were
warmly thanked but we were not invited in.

Florence, August:

The driveway, leading to the Villa Ciappi, was lined with
cedars which filled the air with a resinous fragrance. Beyond,
under a hot beige sky, could be seen the gleam of blossoming
shrubbery and flowers. We never learned whether or not the
occupants of the villa were the owners, but they showed no
hesitation in directing us up a winding staircase to a vantage
point in the tower. There, bathed in the morning sunshine,
lay the great city, engulfed by war and divided by opposing
forces, but still, and relatively silent, in the shimmering heat.
A taut anxious silence, broken by occasional salvos of distant
artillery, the high-pitched chatter of automatic weapons, and
the whipcrack of single rounds of rifle fire.

To the right of our position appeared the familiar facade
of San Miniato al Monte, partly hidden by cypress trees.

Shell-bursts settled about the saddle in the hills, to the east of Fiesole. Almost hidden by the wooded hill of San Leonardo, the crenellated top of the Cambio Tower was just visible. The cupola of the Doumo bulked beside the Shepherds' Tower, the golden orb surmounting the lantern and gleaming like a first magnitude star in the morning sunshine. Further to the left was San Lorenzo, and the tall campanile of Santa Maria Novello created a strong vertical near the station.

The view did not reveal the river. The tragedy of the bridges was mercifully hidden by the dark woods of cypress and ilex below us. The bridges had been blown a day or two earlier, one of the more barbarous acts of a vindictive enemy.

The scene before us recalled Vasari's panoramic fresco on the walls of the old palace. In that busy descriptive work the same foreground which we now overlooked bristled with the brave encampment of the Prince of Orange. From our cockloft today not a soldier was to be seen, yet we knew that they far outnumbered the army led by the Prince. Today's troops were hidden, even as we were hidden. As we watched, another sniper's rifle snapped and the ricochet whined above the dark luxury of the Boboli Gardens.

My objective was to paint a picture of Florence beset by war. Having appreciated the general situation, I was anxious to approach more closely to the river to see what remained of the bridges. Captain L. A. Wrinch and I returned to the jeep and started off toward the Porta San Giorgio. Edging cautiously down the walled lane of the Via Leonardo we reached an iron gateway which I judged to be the Fort Belvedere. A young woman answered our vigorous knocking. We were not at the Fort, but we were at liberty to observe the city from the upper porch of their villa. Delighted by this courtesy, we followed through a charming living-room in which hung what appeared to be an eighteenth century English family portrait, and up a hallway lined with Clouet prints, to a dark staircase which led to a glassed-in porch, disclosing a thrilling and more intimate view of the city's centre.

It was a fascinating view, but still not what I wanted. I envisaged the town with the river in the foreground, showing the demolished bridges. Our new friends suggested the Piazzale Michelangiolo, a reasonable suggestion, but might we not present an obvious target for enemy snipers? Acquainted with the nature of my mission, the ladies readily offered their porch, should it prove the most desirable location, but I must see the bridges.

Captain Wrinch asked where the picture gallery was. It was everywhere, but I pointed out the Uffizi, empty, I had been told, during this trouble. A wise precaution, the precious acquisitiveness of the Reichmarshal being an additional risk to the possibility of damage. On our way north we had heard various rumours of the "liberation" of masterpieces. It was said that many had been found in the Pisa valley castle once owned by the late Sir George Sitwell. Much of the city's statuary was rumoured to be safe in a tunnel near Incisa, the Ghiberti bronze doors from the Baptistry crated and encased in concrete, as was Michelangelo's famous statue, "La Notte." Little seemed to be known of the pictures. What we heard we took to be largely wishful thinking on the part of our informants, but it was said that they were distributed in eight separate hideouts, both north and south of the Arno, with three of these thought to be now in Allied hands.

We withdrew from our vantage point, descended to the courtyard, and drove carefully back to the Via Galileo. Regaining this garden thoroughfare and wisely concluding that a jeep moving along such an exposed roadway would offer too attractive a target, something like a clay rabbit in a shooting gallery, we sought out some deep shade, harboured and demobilized the vehicle, and proceeded toward our objective on foot.

The Via Galileo was empty of traffic but an occasional pedestrian lay prostrate in cover below the privet hedge that bounds the footpath, signalling us frantically to keep out of sight, not so much in consideration of our safety, I fear, as because we might draw fire on their hiding place as we passed. Occasional shots rang out, and in the more exposed sections of the road we moved carefully but without difficulty. It was not until we had reached the long flight of steps leading to the church of San Miniato al Monte that we encountered what we took to be fixed-line fire. We were hidden from the city, and looking up at that glistening mosaic which centres the tympanum, when suddenly our interest was rudely diverted by the chatter of a Spandau. Nothing is more disconcerting than the spatter of lead as it zips through foliage and vegetation. We lay very close to the steps for some time before edging over toward what used to be a restaurant behind the Piazzale Michelangiolo. By that time we were thoroughly alerted to the delicacy of the situation. A British Corporal commanding an observation post advised against our going out onto the Piazzale, but suggested that I might see the river and the bridges if I crawled out behind some sandbags that had been piled behind one side of the balustrade.

There was the Arno, flowing around the wrecked piers of its bridges. The Ponte Vecchio stood deserted and alone, its approaches gone. But what shook me most was the fact that the slender arches of the Ponte Santa Trinata had disappeared. This bridge had been distinguished for its linear elegance and structural power. Now I could see only the heaps of debris, emerging from the river between the massive piers. It was Michelangelo himself who had sketched the original design and inspired Ammanati to build those sprightly arches that had seemed to belie the fact that they were constructed of stone. Now they had been blown to fragments and distributed on the muddy bottom of the Arno, a depressing discovery and one which did not inspire me to paint, even had sketching been possible with a key-hole view and from a decidedly uncomfortable prone position. I wriggled carefully and slowly back to the "O-pip" and Wrinch and I withdrew by the same route to the location of our harboured vehicle.

Back at the Canadian encampment, eleven kilometres
south of Florence, in the lovely valley of the Greve River,
we made preparations to join the main body of the Division
near Perugia. I recall that as we tried to sleep that night,
we heard a tipsy soldier making his way slowly through the
tent lines singing:

> Give me a horse
> A great big horse
> And let me yell Ya-hoo!

Withdrawal:

The engine run-up completed, the plane surged across the
airfield with a deafening roar. The runway fell away quickly,
the landing gear folded neatly into the wing and, as we
banked, the world seemed to rise on its edge.

There below was the great city, gyrating slowly with the
Michelangelo dome at its hub, the Tiber curving gently
through a catalogue of memories old and new, like a bright
ribbon through white hair. The pine cones, the waxen flowers,
the inlays of jasper and lapis lazuli, the royal figure of Aneas,
striding through the stanzas of Virgil, the shrill of swallows
in the evening, the horns of Moses. The Rome of the Republic
and of the Emperors, of Ovid and Juvenal and Cicero. The
sonorous whisper of the pines, the spiral lantern of Sant Evo.
Peter martyred, Charlemagne crowned, the splash of
fountains, the finger of Almighty God. The Pamphili, the
Borghese, the Conti. Acanthus springing greenly from the
ancient soil of the Forum. These and countless other images
crowded the mind as Rome dissolved in mist and gave way
to the glaring floods of the Pontine marshes.

Like myself, the other military passengers relaxed as
much as the situation permitted, no doubt thinking, as I was,
how pleasantly cool it was up here compared with the dense
brassy heat we had left on the ground below.

It had been an infernal rush that morning. Campbell
Tinning had brought me a carafe of precious drinking water,

in which I had performed my ablutions before consuming a now-forgotten breakfast. Outside, cadmium sunlight struck horizontally through the plane trees as we crossed the Piazza Cinquecento on our way to pick up my travelling companion, Major Perce Lailey, at the fabulous "A" mess. Although it was early, a sultry heat hung heavily in the morning air. There has always been heat here in August. As we left the ancient walls behind and hurried under the arched dapple of the Via Flaminia, I experienced very real regret that this stirring assignment was ending and that I might be looking at Rome and Italy for the last time.

The hangars at the Littorio airport were an impressive tangle of twisted girders, but the surface of the field had been restored and the runways were perfect. Major Simmons of "Movements" had come down to see us off and chatted gaily as we weighed our baggage. We had a longish wait before our flight was called at 0830 hours. Eighteen service passengers, including Major General Burch of the Indian Army and an American Red Cross girl, queued up at the gangway and twenty minutes later we were airborne.

*   *   *

For the present my service in Italy is at an end. Under the circumstances I cannot but be reflective of all that has taken place since my arrival in the country nearly a year ago. Particularly are my thoughts with those gallant friends who, unlike myself, will not return. One carries the memory of their sacrifice like a banner in one's heart, sees each handsome face, recalls the tone of voice, the laughter, the sense of humour, the sense of duty, the unselfish willingness to give everything for the cause of a free world.

*   *   *

We skirted the Tyrrhenian coast, passing to the west of Gaeta and Formia, and then the familiar horns of the Bay appeared. We lost altitude over Ischia and swept low over

ROUTE 6 AT CASSINO.

DESTROYED PANZERTRUM ON THE ADOLF HITLER LINE.

Posillipo, where Virgil had dwelt. Vesuvius looked grey and silent; lapili from the spring eruption still dusted the southern slopes of the cone and lent a lifeless pallour to that lush vineyard. Capodichino rushed up as we came in for the landing.

Sullen wilting heat poured around us as we walked to the administration building. A nameless "Movements" officer greeted us and was so astonishingly polite and solicitous that we really felt the C.M.F. was sorry to see us leave.

After an hour's wait, and some refreshment, we rose once more into the welcome coolness above Naples. The ancient Toledo wavered at the foot of the Pizzo-Falcone. Sunlight glinted the roof of the San Carlo. The autostrada struck a firm line between Portici and the texture that had been Pompeii. Capri lay under us on our right, a magic island floating in an uninterrupted void of blue, its pink volcanic crags overlain with gauzy mist, discreetly hiding those capricious delights that thrive in its fair climates. The rocky headlands of the Sorrento peninsula trailed behind, clusters of white villas marking Positano and Amalfi, and with these last impressions mingling pleasantly in the mind, we were out of sight of land over the Mediterranean.

The interior of this metal plane was stripped to the ribbing. Military passengers sat facing one another, with their backs to the fuselage, on shallow little jump seats about the size of a dessert plate. Down the middle of the plane was stowed a cargo of crates and miscellaneous package freight, giving the overall impression that one was travelling in an overcrowded railway express car. But no complaints escaped any of us; we knew how fortunate we were. Most of us were on our way to England and all of us were alive and well.

An hour and a half later, we sighted the westerly tip of Sicily near Trapani. Terra cotta coloured islands stood out from the mainland, rimmed with bottle-green water, the sea surface an immense calm, the sky cloudless. We had thought, when we left Naples, that we were headed directly toward

Algiers, but with the sun-baked expanses of Sicily extending into the blue distance, a thread of rumour supported the idea that Tunis might be our next call.

*   *   *

My last day in the hot Roman sunshine had been a hectic one. I had hoped that the packing and labelling of my heavy equipment would be the last exhausting claim on my time, other than picking up my route letter and transportation. I had had it in mind that I might then spend the balance of the day quietly ruminating in one or two favoured locations: lunch at the Villa Valadier, a walk in the Pincio, a brouse around the Piazza Navonna, a shaded seat on the Janiculum, possibly a last look at the Basilica Julia. But none of these selfish pleasures was I able to indulge in. O'Neil, my driver, in spite of having appealed to all the official sources, had been unable to obtain a replacement for the tire we had blown the previous day and since MacDonald was under orders to return to the Division without delay, I thought we had better all try to help. We were no more successful than O'Neil had been until MacDonald met an angel in the form of Captain Watson, Staff Captain "Q." He did not have a new tire, but in exchange for our tattered wreck, he gave us one designed for a station wagon that might get the jeep back to Perugia. I breathed more easily.

I found Eric Harrison in Ward "M," No. 5 Canadian General Hospital, looking very pale and drawn. We both tried hard to muster the gaiety of other meetings but it was too hot, I was too preoccupied, and he was too ill. I told him of my meeting with Tom Allen and how impressed I had been with his battle record with the P.P.C.L.I. and his qualifications as a possible replacement for Sam Hughes. Harrison nodded but made no comment, as he sipped lime juice through a glass straw. He inquired about my transportation arrangements and mustered a thin smile as he shook my hand and asked me to convey his greetings to all and sundry in London. I flattered myself that he was sad to see me leave and took my departure from the Collegio Militare and withdrew across the Ponte Mazzini into the city.

*   *   *

An abysmal blue void of space surrounded us briefly, but it seemed a surprisingly short time before the emptiness yielded a distant trace of blue which grew rapidly and resolved itself into the bold headland of Cap Bon; the rumour had been right. We lost altitude over the Gulf of Tunis, the wake of many vessels scuffing its surface, a white rim of breakers surrounding the islands of Zembra and Zembretta. A landing wheel emerged out of the wing as we descended over a blinding succession of white, flat-roofed buildings, mosques, minarets, and bazaars. The plane banked steeply and turned toward the east, as the runways of El Awina airport rose to meet us.

The glare and heat on the tarmac was appalling after the coolness of the upper air. We squinted and mopped as we climbed into the truck which took us to a mess hall for refreshment. We were advised to stick together and to remain in the building as our flight would be resumed in thirty minutes. There was evidently going to be no time to have a look at Tunis.

At 1400 hours we were airborne again, rising over small sandy holdings. Tiny toy-block houses had some red crop, possibly tomatoes, drying on their flat roofs. The air was bumpy over an untidy snaggle of low flower-pot red hills, covered with irregular groves of olive trees, looking like cloves stuck into an Easter ham. Our passenger list had been reduced to eight, Lailey, Taggart and myself the only sur-vivors of the Roman party. Five U.S. Air Force pilots had been added, together with a tumble of new packing cases which we noted were destined for Casablanca.

We cut across another peninsula and there below was the magnificent crescent of Stora Bay, Cap de Fer, which I had

painted last September, the cork forest, then Philippeville
itself. The trials and delights of our stay on this fabulous
cote d'azûr returned to me as I gazed south in the hope of
seeing Constantine, but the ground haze in that direction was
too dense. The tent lines were gone; the cork forest appeared
to have been returned to the lizards and the birds and its
accustomed silence.

*   *   *

Stora Bay sent me back once more, thumbing over the
pages of an astounding experience. My leave-taking at
Divisional Headquarters had made clear the deep attachments
I had made there. The Division, to use again that misleading
term, was "At rest" in an encampment near Perugia. It
was a Sunday when I sat in "E" mess for the last time.
Innumerable church bells tinkled and tolled on the great
Umbrian plain below. The olives were almost full grown
and the still-green grape clusters were developing a slight
blush. Summer was full-blown and a great heat descended,
burning and ripening. Familiar conversations buzzed, as I
looked around the table and noted the eager young faces
laughing and wise-cracking. Few of the originals remained,
the turnover was continuous.

I went over to the Divisional Quartermaster and turned
in all my web, my pistol, ammunition, respirator, and helmet.
There was a certain finality and sense of separation about
parting with such familiar equipment. I felt positively naked
without it. Then came the handshaking, the warm friendly
confidences, the telephone numbers and messages to wives and
sweethearts in England.

Lt. Col. M. P. "Pat" Bogert, the G.S.O.1., walked over to
the G.O.C.'s compound with me. General Vokes received us
with a ruddy smile. He sat sweltering behind a deskful of
paper, dealing out death to innumerable flies with a scarlet
horsehair switch. He called for his steward and ordered
refreshment. Serving at my level, there is little opportunity
for an officer to become acquainted with a G.O.C., but in the

ten months I had been under his command I had developed
a great admiration for this forthright Canadian. "Chris"
Vokes bristled with rousing vigour. His very appearance
radiated aggressive energy and combined extraordinary
powers of determined military leadership with a Rabelaisian
sense of humour and a reflective and cultured mind. These
impressions had been confirmed when I made a sketch portrait
of him at Raviscanina the previous June, on which occasion
he had discussed literature and history, while making decisions
on a variety of military problems with his staff. Now, as we
sipped tea, he told of meeting a middle-aged Italian peasant
inside our lines, wearing the ribbon of the Canadian Volunteer
Service Medal. When he accosted the man and asked him
what he was doing in the camp area, and where he got the
ribbon, the man replied that a Canadian soldier had given it
to his wife for doing his laundry. The Field Security were
still investigating . . . He rose from his chair, shook my hand
warmly, and I left the Division twenty minutes later.

Our route skirted Perugia. As we approached and passed
Assisi, I peered earnestly at that now familiar cluster of
tiled buildings on the hillside and at the square campanile of
San Francesco. At Spoleto we were diverted over a mountain
detour which brought us back on to our route beneath the
impressive falls of the Nera River near Terni. The great
river gushed over a precipice high above us and cascaded
down over craggy rocks into the deep canyon, through which
the road wound. Narni stood high on its hill. Then, clearing
the mountains we descended onto the Roman campagna. It
had been an extremely hot day. Just as a consoling mirage
of cool refreshment buoyed our flagging spirits, we blew our
left rear tire.

　　　　　*　　　　　*　　　　　*

We passed well out to sea over Bougie Bay, and then over
the town of Bougie itself. The terrain below was now barren
and mountainous, vast sandy hills, wild and uncultivated,
with a very sparse unknown forestry, browns, tans, greys, no

other chromatic accent. Beyond Dellys we brought up a pattern of cultivation, roads appeared and multiplied, the ordered abstractions of an airfield suggested a metropolitan area, and then to starboard was Algiers, shining whitely in the afternoon sun. Beyond it, out to sea, was an eastbound convoy, steaming strongly toward Italy.

Leaving Algiers behind, we moved inland again, down the arid valley of the Cheliff with the ragged peaks of the Du Dahra Zaccar massif to the north and the L'Ouarsenis to the south. Shortly before six, Oran came into view and, as had been predicted, we came down for fuel and orders. Our ferry pilots were first out. They know these places like the backs of their hands and we followed them to another snack bar where French only was spoken. The heat on the ground was still powerful. The food was rather odd but welcome, the beverages, a sharp, sweet lemonade, or coffee; we had both. Something the vendor said as he handed us the food made me suddenly realize the significance of Oran in recent Anglo-French relations, but we ignored the remark and joined our travelling companions in their excited enthusiasms over the local rumour concerning the progress of "Anvil." The news, if true, was spectacular: a hundred mile front had been opened up between Marseilles and Nice and all primary objectives had been achieved. We finished our food in a friendly glow of good fellowship.

Besides the news from France, we learned that we were to proceed immediately to Casablanca and that the trans-Atlantic night flight was being held at that point for our American ferry pilots. We bundled back into the Dakota, refreshed and exuberant over this surfeit of good fortune.

As the sun declined the surface contours of the terrain below us were thrown into striking relief. We were headed inland, across a bleached desert that looked at times like the South Dakota badlands. There was no cultivation, just a reddish-brown emptiness, deeply eroded by dry, winding gullies. A poor isolated olive tree suggested that possibly this arid land had known other and better days, but the general

effect was of looking down on crinkled brown wrapping paper.
To the south were stark, bleak, slag-heap ranges, devoid of
vegetation. Occasionally a tiny pocket handkerchief of faded
green would appear with the impact of a traffic signal on a
dark night. Suddenly a sprawl of buildings clustered about a
single track railway and, just as suddenly, was gone. This
we learned was Oudjda. Then the desert took over again and
we roared on and on over the vast emptiness of Morocco.

Our ferry pilot friends were asleep on the floor. They
are a gay happy-go-lucky crew. They say little about their
experiences and we have learned not to ask, but it was clear
from their conversations that they were on their way home
from Burma to the United States to pick up another flight
of bombers. What never seems to occur to them is the
overwhelming miracle of their service; time and space on a
global scale seem to be of no greater concern to them than
commuting to the business man. Thinking, when one is flying
over Tunisia, of picking up one's laundry in Dallas, Texas,
would seem to suggest that a new age of global thought and
movement is already established. A journey from Texas to
Singapore no longer has the connotations of even twenty
years ago; here is the restless, frenetically mobile generation
of a very new world.

Over Taza the scene changed, we entered a rugged
mountain pass at about nine thousand feet. Below, the
Innaouen River twisted and tossed busily, mocking the single
track railway which followed apprehensively behind. To
the south rose the great Moyen Atlas, memorializing that
Homeric colossus who supports the pillars of heaven. One
of the ferry pilots leaned over and shouted in my ear, "They
got lions in them thar hills." I nodded acknowledgment and
passed the surprising information along to Taggart. To the
north were the Rif Mountains of Spanish Morocco, a saw-
tooth range that seemed to be associated in my mind with
perpetual brigandry and tribal violence. The sun was getting
low and a ruddy light intensified the wild aspect of the planet
below us. At the same time I felt chilly for the first time since

last spring and began to doubt the wisdom of making the flight in K.D. shorts and a bush shirt.

Central Morocco opened out into a wide agricultural plain as the picturesque and ancient oriental city of Fez came into view. It covered a wide area and appeared to be clearly divided between a conglomerate kasbah and a planned and boulevarded modern city. Longing for some form of perceptive aid which would give us the miraculous power of witnessing the life which teemed below, we peered down, conjuring in our minds the colourful caravans of the Barbary trade and those from far away Timbuktu on the Niger. Might not that square contain a great Mosque where the approaching sunset will be the scene of worship, the walled area a Sultan's palace where, even at this moment he may be contemplating the delights of an evening in his seraglio, the weird pipings, the jingle of anklets and bracelets as the dancers stamp and whirl . . . or might there instead be dinner jackets and cummerbunds and an enlightened discussion of the course of the war in Europe?

Thirty air miles further west we passed over Meknes, a similar native quarter, and, removed a bit, a handsomely planned modern town. The sun set and darkness came quickly, but not before we had seen the great wall of the Atlantic, rising up like a mighty genie before us. We all looked in wonder at this stupendous ocean and I felt sure, as I looked at Lailey, that he shared the thought that was passing through my mind. This same great ocean touches Canada's shores and I am sure we were sharing the implications of that fact. Although we were viewing it in the growing darkness above Morocco, there was profound solace in the thought.

My ears clicked in the darkness and it was obvious that we were losing altitude over a wide lighted area. "Seat belts!" —and the marvels of a lighted city twinkled below. I looked at my watch; it was five minutes to ten. There was no blackout in Casablanca. As we banked over the city, myriad lights marked streets and buildings and headlights of cars could be seen, moving in and about them. The landing lights went on and I saw that the flaps and landing wheels were already down. Runway markers flashed by the windows and we touched down at Cazes air base.

*   *   *

I was being quietly retrospective in a corner of the waiting-room at Cazes. Reflectively I recalled that only a brief year ago I had been at St. Eval. It seemed like a decade, so much had happened since.

A year ago I had been in Cornwall with the 2nd Battalion, Royal Canadian Engineers. They were extending the capacity of an existing airfield at St. Eval, about ten miles from Newquay, and I was endeavouring to translate their activities into some form of visual record. I knew at that time that it was the ultimate intention of the Historical Section to assign war artists to Canadian units on a fighting front. Ogilvie was already in the Mediterranean so I gave little thought to the possibility of being sent to that theatre myself. Although alternatives had not yet appeared at that time, it had occurred to me that I might easily have to await the opening of a front somewhere in northern Europe. Security at C.M.H.Q. was good and I actually knew nothing about an overseas assignment until the afternoon when Colonel C. P. Stacey had called me to his office and told me to report to Aldershot next day. That had been on the 31st August last. . .

It interested me that as I sat there in Casablanca my thinking should suddenly have become concerned with England, with St. Eval. Captain G. D. Gibson, the Toronto architect had been the adjutant there, and Colonel W. A. Capell the O. C., and the weather had been just its damp Cornish self. Little remained of the village, except the church. The whole area had been expropriated in order that huge bomber airfields could be built on the high contours of Blackmoor. The Canadians were extending the runways so that the very largest transoceanic aircraft could land and take off from this most westerly site in England.

It was that massive airview of the Atlantic that had done
it. A sudden dislocation of ideas and values had occurred as
that great field of recollected associations rose out of the west.
The Italian experience ended there. It was now a complete
and unforgettable part of personal history. What filled my
mind at the moment was the fact that, barring accident,
tomorrow morning would bring me once more to England.

At St. Eval there had been two airfields, occupying
adjoining high contours, the second St. Mawgans. They were
situated just a short walk from the rugged coastal feature of
Bedruthan Steps, an impressive coastline of impregnable red
rock, upon which the mighty swells of the Atlantic crashed
incessantly.

The old church had fascinated me. It was an ancient place
of worship with traces of Saxon building and a Norman font,
but built chiefly in the perpendicular style. The principal
external feature was an embattled western tower said to have
been built by the merchants of Bristol in the 17th century,
ostensibly as a worthy addition to the building, but actually
to provide their sailing masters with a fixed landmark. There
were still traces of the whitewash in the mortar joints of this
sailing marker, painted at the expense of these merchants
from time to time. Today the church was the only remnant
of a snug little Cornish village, the peel of its bells replaced
now by the thrumming vibrations of armed aircraft as
Lancasters and Liberators took off for missions deep in the
heartlands of continental Europe.

*   *   *

Lailey nudged me as the public address system instructed
personnel travelling to the United Kingdom on Flight 206
to present themselves and baggage for inspection and weighing. Our ferry pilots had long since wished us "Happy
Landings" and disappeared into the darkness of the airfield,
bound for the U. S. A.

On first landing at Cazes, we had been loaded into a command vehicle and driven to a U.S. Air Force dining-hall at the other end of the huge base. Following an attractive and satisfying meal, we had been returned to the administration building, been placed on the nominal roll of passengers for Flight 206, and then given a very comprehensive briefing by a U.S. Technical Sergeant, who described the Mae West, how it should be worn and inflated, spoke of the rubber life boats and how they should be inflated and launched, and ended with the sinister caution, "Now remember, no more than five of you guys can get into any one boat!" We were a bit shaken by this admonition. One of the new passengers claimed that the enemy sent out night interceptors regularly for the sole purpose of bringing down Flight 206. That might be so, but we had no premonition of disaster and dismissed his dismal pessimism with a shrug.

The baggage examination and weighing was perfunctory and we returned wearily to our seats. We had been on the move for eighteen hours and it was only the promise of England in the morning that kept us awake. A crowd stood around a gigantic map of Europe, on which the progress of "Overlord" and "Anvil" were recorded. We had looked at it with great interest earlier, now we just looked. As we looked, I saw an attractive and jaunty little person, wearing an American wedge hat and uniform, walking smartly toward us. What attracted me first was the row of unit badges sewn on her sleeve, there seemed to be a score of them. When I took in the other features of this trim little figure, I recognized Lily Pons, the brilliant coloratura soprano. Fatigue seemed to fall away from my companions, as it did from me, as she smiled, seemingly toward us, before disappearing into the outer darkness. She had created a miracle of resuscitation, conversation was resumed everywhere. I had last seen her on the stage of the Metropolitan. Was it in the role of Gilda or Lakmé? I could only recall the bell-like clarity and beauty of her voice. What was she doing in Casablanca? Lailey seemed to recall that she and her husband, André Kostelanetz, had recently appeared in Rome?

"Flight 206 loading at gate 12!" We pulled ourselves together, put on trench coats, and followed the other military passengers out into the darkness. There, with its engines already turning over, was the dark silhouette of a Liberator. We assembled at the foot of an aluminum ladder and, as our names were called, climbed up into the lighted interior. Unlike the Dakota, in which we had travelled from Rome, this ship was fitted with all the comforts of a regular mainliner. We relaxed in the embrace of seats of unparalleled luxury, adjusted seat belts, and with the last man aboard, the door slammed shut and the plane taxied off to the starting runway. There we remained an interminable time, carefully running up each of the four engines, until suddenly they roared in terrifying unison and we were off into the night at 0035 hours.

*   *   *

We had seen nothing but the lights of Casablanca. Cazes was an efficiently administered U.S. Air Base. We might have been at Englewood or Boeing Field. England was our destination and we were already well out over the Atlantic on the final leg of our journey.

The Atlantic! How many times had I looked out over that great sea? From Lunenburg, through a forest of masts and spars. From St. Margaret's Bay, with that great scatter of monolithic boulders framing the boiling surf. From Halifax, with mewing gulls circling the sheds and derricks above the toneless clang of bellbuoys and the thump of sirens. From the decks of ships, as Mother Carey's Chickens skipped from wave crest to wave crest, the vessel creaking like a corsetted duchess as she rolled with the swell, or perhaps idly watching the sludgy salt spray descend into the spume with the sound and weight of gravel.

I must have slept, for as I roused myself I saw that it was already seven o'clock. I cautiously lifted a corner of the blackout curtain to find the exhaust manifolds a fiery red, and the sun risen into a confused sub-fusc sky. Occasional rents in the cloud field, fantastically beautiful in the early light, revealed the serene calm of the ocean far below. Another break and I glimpsed a rugged coastline and a margin of surf.

Rumour had it that we would land at Londonderry or Prestwick. It mattered little. We had land below us and we would soon know. The cloud field showed signs of breaking up and then the coast appeared again. We were much lower. A town appeared with a scarp-like row of buildings and an esplanade facing a wide stretch of white sand, behind it the greenest of green fields. It looked familiar, surprisingly like Newquay. I was excited. It must be the Cornish coast below us. In a few minutes my conviction was confirmed. There below us was St. Eval church, and the airfield I knew so well.

"Seat Belts!" was signalled from the flight deck as we banked and nosed down through ragged cloud. Landing gear appeared out of the wings, wheels spinning merrily. We emerged low over England, a lush revelation of intimate greens and browns and the yellow-gold of stooked grain. Was it only yesterday that we had flown over the arid deserts of Tunisia and Morocco? The tires of the landing wheels chirped an abrasive complaint as they gripped the asphalt runway and we rolled swiftly and quietly to a full stop.